A Physiological
Basis for
Personality Traits

A Physiological Basis For Personality Traits

A NEW THEORY OF PERSONALITY

By

DAVID LESTER, Ph.D.
Richard Stockton State College
Pomona, New Jersey

CHARLES C THOMAS · PUBLISHER
Springfield · Illinois · U.S.A.

Published and Distributed Throughout the World by
CHARLES C THOMAS · PUBLISHER
BANNERSTONE HOUSE
301-327 East Lawrence Avenue, Springfield, Illinois, U.S.A.

© *1974, by* CHARLES C THOMAS · PUBLISHER
ISBN 0-398-03078-2
Library of Congress Catalog Card Number: 73-19613

With THOMAS BOOKS *careful attention is given to all details of manufacturing and design. It is the Publisher's desire to present books that are satisfactory as to their physical qualities and artistic possibilities and appropriate for their particular use.* THOMAS BOOKS *will be true to those laws of quality that assure a good name and good will.*

Printed in the United States of America
H-2

Library of Congress Cataloging in Publication Data

Lester, David, 1942-
  A physiological basis for personality traits.

  1. Personality. 2. Psychology, physiological. 3. Psychology, Pathological.
I. Title. [DNLM: 1. Personality. 2. Personality disorders. 3. Psychophysiology.
BF698.9.B5 L642p 1974]
BF698.L397   155.2'34   73-19613
ISBN 0-398-03078-2

The classification of personality types and disordered

behavior by autonomic nervous system balance

P-types	*S-types*
augmenters	*N-subtype*
alcoholics	paranoid
schizophrenics	murderers
congenitally deaf	mesomorphs
sharpeners	anger-in and anxiety reactions to stress
hypochondriacs	
introverts	
males	*A-subtype*
ectomorphs	endomorphs
dysthymics	suicides
field independence	manic-depressives
sensitizers	anger-out reaction to stress

Presently Undifferentiable
reducers
thrill seekers
levelers
brain-damaged
delinquents
self-mutilators
smokers
lung cancer patients
lepers
extraverts
females
hysterics
repressers
field dependence

CONTENTS

PART ONE
INTRODUCTION

PART TWO
TWO TRAIT THEORIES OF PERSONALITY

PART THREE
THREE TRAIT THEORIES

PART FOUR
PSYCHOPATHOLOGY

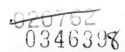

PART FIVE
SEX DIFFERENCES IN BEHAVIOR

PART SIX
CONCLUSIONS

A Physiological
Basis for
Personality Traits

PART ONE **INTRODUCTION**

CHAPTER 1 **INTRODUCTION**

THIS BOOK is an attempt to suggest a physiological basis for a number of diverse personality traits and theories. It presents a synthesis of existing research that has, hitherto, been seen as disparate and unrelated. I have been struck in my perusal of the psychological literature how inter-related these researches and theories are, and yet how little commonality is usually noted. A quick glance at the table of contents for this book will show the reader how many psychological dimensions will be related to each other, ranging from personality traits such as extraversion/introversion, to behavior disorders, and to sex differences in performance.

The choice of a psychological basis for this unification and synthesis might be taken to imply that I have a firm belief in constitutional theories of personality. This is not so. Although it is likely, or even certain, that physiological processes do underlie many psychological behaviors and traits, the choice of a physiological basis was not made because of this belief. Rather, I came to see how a particular physiological dimension provided a means of integrating the disparate research. Indeed, now that I have finished the task, I am unable to see any other basis, physiological or psychological, for integrating the material.

Perhaps the fact that a physiological process was able to provide a basis for the integration of so many different psychological dimensions points to the fact that physiological processes do play a more important role in personality than we appear to realize. I use the word "appear" intentionally. It is, I think, true to say that most psychologists would accept the notion that the physiology of our bodies does affect our behavior. But the research that psychologists conduct on personality rarely comes to grips with this physiological foundation.

A PHYSIOLOGICAL BASIS FOR PERSONALITY

The physiological basis that I have used to integrate the psychological research and theories is the autonomic nervous system, with its two major divisions (the sympathetic nervous system and the parasympathetic nervous system) and with its two major subdivisions of the sympathetic nervous system (the adrenalin and the noradrenalin reactions).* I do not claim of course, to be the first psychologist to note the relevance of these dimensions to behavior. Those who have hinted at their relevance will be acknowledged throughout this book. However, no-one has yet seen the possible ramifications of these physiological processes for the wide range of human behavior described in this book.

THE AUTONOMIC NERVOUS SYSTEM, EMOTION, AND PERSONALITY

Many psychologists accept the notion that the autonomic nervous system plays a role in the appearance of emotional behavior and perhaps too in the subjective experience of emotions. The notion that the autonomic nervous system may affect personality is not so readily accepted. However, the idea is not completely without historical basis.

Galen (1952) developed Hippocrates' four-fold classificatory system of personality and hinted at the relationship between the personality traits and the underlying emotions upon which they are based. The four personalities (sanguine, phlegmatic, choleric, and melancholic) can be reduced to two dimensions: the intensity of the emotion that can be aroused in the individual and the speed with which that emotion can be aroused (see Wundt, 1903).

		the intensity of the emotion	
		weak	strong
the speed	fast	sanguine	choleric
of arousal	slow	phlegmatic	melancholic

A modern psychologist who has considered the relationship between personality and emotions is Plutchik (1962). Plutchik has attempted to classify the different emotions into a rational system and he posited the existence of eight primary emotions. These eight primary emotions

---

*I prefer these terms over epinephrine and norepinephrine.

can then be combined to form mixed or complex emotions. Plutchik noted that many terms for emotions represent feeling states that seem relatively persistent. Emotions such as pride, optimism, and anxiety are often long-lasting states and they are commonly seen as personality traits. Plutchik argued that the formation of personality traits was related to the development of mixed emotions, since mixed emotions involve some degree of conflict.

The notion that persisting situations which produce mixed emotions also produce personality traits is not without precedent. Plutchik quotes Fenichel (1946):

> Character traits are the precipitates of instinctual conflicts. . . . In character attitudes, conflicts between impulses and fears may be relatively frozen. . . . This then is the situation. Once there was a conflict. The individual withdrew from this struggle by means of a permanent ego alteration. The forces that at one time opposed each other are now wasted in the useless and rigid defensive attitudes of the ego; the conflict has become latent.

To illustrate his thesis, Plutchik gave a list of personality traits to college students and to high school teachers and asked them to pick the emotions involved in each personality trait from a list of primary emotions that he gave them. His judges showed a high degree of agreement. Some examples of the choices of the judges are given below:

Personality Trait	Emotion-Component	
	First Choice	*Second Choice*
sarcastic	annoyance	loathing
cruel	rage	loathing
shy	timidity	fear
servile	fear	acceptance
hopeful	anticipation	pleasure

Although it is possible to study the phenomenology of emotions on a purely subjective level, many investigators have studied the physiological responses that accompany emotions. Investigators such as James (1884) and Schachter (1971) see emotions as basically physiological patterns of responses that are accompanied by particular "feeling." (Schachter stresses also a cognitive input that joins with the physiological input to produce the subjective experience.) With this point of view, it is easy to conceptualize personality traits as long-standing characteristic ways of responding physiologically to particular stimuli (internal and external), that are also accompanied by particular subjective feelings.

It should be noted in passing that some investigators do focus upon physiological underpinnings of personality. Eysenck (1964) has looked to inhibition in the central nervous system as a physiological foundation. Sheldon (1942) has looked to physique. However, the autonomic nervous system has not often been seen as a possible physiological foundation. (Incidentally, I might note that I shall argue that the autonomic nervous system provides a better foundation for both Eysenck's theory and Sheldon's than the physiological processes that they chose.)

In order to pursue my thesis, it is necessary first to describe the operation of the autonomic nervous system in some detail. The following chapter is therefore concerned with this task.

REFERENCES

Eysenck, H. J.: *Crime And Personality*. Boston, Houghton-Mifflin, 1964.

Fenichel, O.: *The Psychoanalytic Theory Of Neurosis*. London, Routledge and Kegan Paul, 1946.

Galen: On the natural faculties. In Kutchins, R. M. (Ed.): *Great Books Of The Western World, Volume 10*. Chicago, Encyclopaedia Britannica, 1952, pp. 163-215.

James, W.: What is an emotion. *Mind, 9*: 188-205, 1884.

Plutchik, R.: *The Emotions*. New York, Random House, 1962.

Schachter, S.: *Emotions, Obesity, and Crime*. New York, Academic, 1971.

Sheldon, W. H.: *The Varieties Of Temperament*. New York, Harper and Row, 1942.

Wundt, W.: *Grundzuge der Physiologischen Psychologie*. Leipzig, W. Englemann, 1903.

CHAPTER 2   THE AUTONOMIC NERVOUS SYSTEM*

SINCE THE central thesis of this book is centered around the notion that individual differences in personality and behavior are related to the ways in which individuals differ in the functioning of their autonomic nervous systems, it is necessary to inquire a little into the autonomic nervous system. What is it and how does it function?

The autonomic nervous system regulates the visceral functions, that is, the functioning of organs and tissues. The autonomic nervous system controls the glands and smooth muscles, in contrast to the somatic nervous system which is concerned with sensory inputs from and control of skeletal (or striped) muscles. For example, nerve impulses commanding the smooth muscles of the gastrointestinal tract to contract are transmitted via the autonomic nervous system, whereas nerve impulses commanding the striped muscles in the arm to contract are transmitted via the somatic nervous system. In the periphery of the body, the autonomic and somatic nervous systems are separate anatomically, physiologically, and to some extent pharmacologically. The two systems are less clearly separated in the central nervous system. The word "autonomic" means functioning independently, and it is generally true to say that control of the autonomic nervous system is not under conscious control. (Recently, there have been some successful attempts in trying to train people to exert conscious control over their autonomic nervous system [Miller, 1969], but the results have not been easily replicable.)

The autonomic nervous system consists of two parts: the sympathetic (or thoracicolumbar) division and the parasympathetic (or craniosacral) division. The terms thoracicolumbar and craniosacral refer to the locations in the spinal cord from which the neurons emerge

---

*This chapter draws heavily on the writings of Grossman (1967) and Leukel (1972).

and enter (save for the cranial component, the nerves of which come directly from the brain).

The two divisions of the autonomic nervous system differ in the chemicals (sometimes called neurohumors) that are involved in the synaptic transmission of nervous impulses. The sympathetic system uses both acetylcholine (the cholinergic system, which is preganglionic) and noradrenalin (the adrenergic system, which is postganglionic). On the other hand, the parasympathetic system uses only acetylcholine and so is totally cholinergic.

It is important to note that the parasympathetic and sympathetic systems both have a supply of motor fibres to the smooth muscles and glands. The sympathetic and parasympathetic systems have, in general, opposed effects on the viscera, though not always. For example, the sympathetic system speeds up and the parasympathetic system slows down the heart beat. The sympathetic system is diffusely organized and tends to be aroused as a whole system. The parasympathetic system is discretely organized and influences only a few visceral structures at a time. The two systems can, however, interact. For example, widespread sympathetic system innervation stimulates more widespread parasympathetic system reactions. Thus, the result is a continually changing balance between the two systems in their effects on the viscera.

Sympathetic system excitation has the following effect: arteries contract and relax in different locations, such that blood is diverted from the digestive system to the somatic muscles in order to fuel their activity; heart rate and blood pressure rise; breathing rate increases and bronchial tubes to the lungs dilate; sweating increases to cool the body; sphincters contract to shut off digestion; and digestive contractions of stomach and intestine cease. In contrast, parasympathetic system excitation slows heart rate and respiration, diverts blood from somatic muscles to the digestive system, increases digestive processes, and inhibits sweating.

Drugs can be used to stimulate, mimic, or enhance the activity of the autonomic nervous system: these drugs are called sympathomimetic and parasympathomimetic drugs. Drugs that block the transmission of impulses in the autonomic nervous system are called sympatholytic (or adrenolytic) and parasympatholytic (or cholinolytic) drugs. The effects of some common drugs are shown in Table 2-I.

Table 2-I. Drugs and the Autonomic Nervous System.

Increased Activation		*Increased Inhibition*	
adrenergic stimulation	cholinergic depression	adrenergic depression	cholinergic stimulation
adrenalin	atropine	reserpine	eserine
dopamine	scopolamine	chlorpromazine	physostigmine
noradrenalin	cholinesterase	monoamine	acetylcholine
glutamic acid	pentamethonium-	oxidase	
gamma-amino-	iodide		
buteric acid			
amphetamine			
(benzedrine sulfate)			
caffeine			
iproniazid			

From Broverman, *et al.* 1968, p. 31.

The part of the central nervous system that appears to be responsible for mediating the autonomic nervous system is the hypothalamus, located in the diencephalon. In general, stimulation of the anterior hypothalamus and preoptic areas tends to excite the parasympathetic system, whereas stimulation of the posterior hypothalamus generally excites the sympathetic system. Exceptions to this clear separation of control centers have however been reported.

AUTONOMIC BALANCE

There is always a balance between sympathetic and parasympathetic arousal. This balance depends upon individual differences in autonomic reactivity and upon current stimulation. Typically, one system predominates over the other. Individuals with a dominant parasympathetic system have excessive salivation, dry palms, a slow heart rate, and high intestinal motility (or a growling stomach). Individuals with a dominant sympathetic system have dry mouths, moist palms, and a fast heart rate at rest. In this connection, we might note that many people would not trust those whose hands are "clammy." People with "clammy" hands have a dominant sympathetic system. Perhaps later in this book, we shall find out why such people are untrustworthy.

The predominance of one system over the other may be short term or it may be persistent. Soldiers in battle will probably have a predominant sympathetic system, but a transient increase in parasympathetic arousal may occur, and result in the soldier defecating in the midst of battle without adequate preparation.

Angina pectoris (a cardiac condition) appears to be related to excessive constriction of the coronary arteries and the effect of this constriction on the heart muscles. This is a result of chronic (or long-standing) parasympathetic stimulation. Peptic ulcers are caused in part by excessive secretion of hydrochloric acid into the stomach and abnormal gastric motility; this again may be the result of chronic parasympathetic stimulation.

Comment

This chapter has served to introduce some of the physiological terms that will occur throughout this book. Now it is time to move onto the development of the thesis. First, the work of Petrie on the personality dimension of augmenting and reducing will be explored for its relationship to the functioning of the autonomic nervous system.

REFERENCES

Broverman, D., Klaiber, E., Kobayashi, Y., and Vogel, W.: Roles of activation and inhibition in sex differences in cognitive abilities. *Psychol Rev, 75:* 23-50, 1968.

Grossman, S.: *A Textbook Of Physiological Psychology.* New York, Wiley, 1967.

Leukel, F.: *Introduction To Physiological Psychology.* St. Louis, Mosby, 1972.

Miller, N. E.: Learning of visceral and glandular responses. *Science, 163:* 434-445, 1969.

PART TWO   # TWO TRAIT THEORIES
            # OF PERSONALITY

CHAPTER 3 REDUCERS AND AUGMENTERS

PETRIE (1967) NOTED that people differ in their modulation of sensory experience. The *reducer* tends subjectively to decrease the intensity of what is sensed; the *augmenter* tends subjectively to increase the intensity of what is sensed; those midway along this dimension of personality, the *moderators,* tend neither to reduce nor to augment what they sense.

Petrie devised a perceptual judgment test of this behavior, in which a blindfolded person feels an object of a given size held between his fingers and then matches the size on a wedged-shaped block. The reducer acts as if the object has been reduced in size after he has felt it for a few minutes (that is, he underestimates its size); the augmenter acts as if the object has increased in size (that is, he overestimates its size).

Performance on this perceptual judgment test is correlated with tolerance for pain, which Petrie measured by noting the difference between the temperature of a thermal stimulus that produced pricking pain and the temperature at which the pain became intolerable. A study by Sweeney (1966) confirmed that these two measures are associated. The tolerance for thermally-caused pain and the perceptual judgment are the two tests used to define the behavior of reducing-augmenting.

PERSONALITY CORRELATES OF REDUCING-AUGMENTING

Petrie has conducted a number of studies to explore the correlates of reducing-augmenting. One major finding was that reducers seem to be similar to extraverts. For example, reducers obtain higher extraversion scores on the Maudsley Personality Inventory (Jensen, 1958) than do augmenters. (They do not differ in neuroticism scores.) Like extraverts, reducers were less able to tolerate sensory deprivation than augmenters.

In a parallel study, Lynn and Eysenck (1961) found that extraverts had a greater tolerance for thermally-caused pain than did introverts.

[15]

Not all investigators, however, confirm this association (e.g. Mumford *et al.*, 1973).

Reducers tend to have less concern about their health than augmenters: they score lower on the hypochondriasis scale of the MMPI, they less often prefer nutritional foods for breakfast, and they smoke more. Reducers were found to have more friends, to be more sociable, to prefer contact sports over noncontact sports, to bite their nails more, to indulge in a greater amount of sexual activity, and to get poorer school grades. Reducers need less sleep, and Petrie speculated that either their day is less stimulating or alternatively that sleep is a greater threat for reducers.

MEDICAL CORRELATES OF REDUCING-AUGMENTING

Petrie studied a group of people who were deaf from birth. They had high augmenting scores and there was a dearth of reducers in the group. People who originally could hear but who became deaf later in life did not differ from normals in reducing-augmenting. Thus, it appears that those who are born without a sensory modality "make up" for its absence by augmenting sensations from other sensory modalities.

Petrie noted that cases exist of persons congenitally indifferent to pain, that is reducers, and Lester (1972) has noted that some cases of self-mutilation have been attributed to congenital indifference to pain. Petrie also noted that those with leprosy appear to be indifferent to pain, and thus are reducers. Petrie presented data from one patient with a phantom limb who was very sensitive to pain (an augmenter). With respect to this, Simmel (1956) has noted that for phantom limbs to appear, the patient must lose the limb suddenly, in which case there is no time to adapt to the loss of sensory input from that limb after amputation. Perhaps time to adapt allows for normal perception of sensory stimuli to persist whereas sudden loss does not permit this, leading the person to compensate by becoming an augmenter. In this case, it would be interesting to compare people who lost sensory input (from amputation, deafness, etc.) after birth gradually with those whose loss was sudden for their reducing-augmenting behavior.

PSYCHOPATHOLOGICAL CORRELATES OF
REDUCING-AUGMENTING

Petrie reported that alcoholics are augmenters (and they were also found to be introverts on the Maudsley Personality Inventory). In general, delinquents were found to be reducers, and there were many extreme reducers among delinquent populations. Petrie speculated that delinquents, as reducers, would need more stimulation from the environment, would need stronger rewards and punishments for these stimuli to be effective, and thus would be poorer learners in normal circumstances. Self-mutilation should be more common in delinquents (and it is). Since afferent input to the central nervous system will be reduced, they should perform poorly in classical conditioning tasks (and they do). They should also fail to empathize with experiences that they do not share. Thus, they may act "sadistically," since they will fail to comprehend suffering from pain.

Petrie found that reducers smoked at an earlier age, enjoyed smoking more, gave it up less often, and expected more often to continue smoking. This may relate to smokers having a greater need for stimulation (see Chapter 16) or to their lowered concern for their own health (see above). In this connection, we might predict that patients with lung cancer will be reducers (see Chapter 16).

In studies of schizophrenics, Petrie came to the conclusion that they were originally augmenters who, under bombardment from excessive sensory stimulation, defensively became reducers. This idea will be discussed in greater detail in Chapter 12.

Silverman (1964a, 1964b) has reported data that suggest that paranoid schizophrenics tend to be augmenters while nonparanoid schizophrenics tend to be reducers. However, Petrie's hypothesis suggests that tests of schizophrenics early in their lives, prior to the onset of their schizophrenic behavior, might produce very different results.

DRUGS AND REDUCING-AUGMENTING

So far, the correlates of reducing-augmenting seem diverse, but the dimension has not been tied down to the autonomic nervous system. Petrie found that chlorpromazine (which depresses adrenergic functioning and so increases parasympathetic dominance) makes people more augmenting, although Petrie based her conclusion on only case studies. On the other hand, aspirin and alcohol changed augmenters into reducers (but had little effect on reducers). Spilker and Callaway (1969) reported that depressants such as alcohol and sodium phenobarbital moved people toward the reducing end of the dimension, but these investigators found no effects from caffeine or methamphetamine. (Spilker and Callaway measured reducing-augmenting in a way that is different from that suggested by Petrie. They measured the visual evoked responses to light stimuli, a measure that they claim taps the same dimension of Petrie's tests.)

Petrie reported that pre-frontal lobotomy also changed augmenters into reducers (and failed most often for extraverts, whom Petrie found to be reducers). Temporal lobectomy had not effect on either reducers or augmenters, as fas as reducing-augmenting is concerned. Petrie noted that audioanalgesia turned augmenters into reducers but had little effect on reducers.

Thus, is appears that augmenters have parasympathetic predominance (that is, they are P-types) while reducers have sympathetic predominance (that is, they are S-types), though only the data on chlorpromazine provides direct evidence for this.

Comment

In conclusion, there is some evidence that the first personality dimension considered in this book, that of reducing-augmenting, is related to the balance between the sympathetic and parasympathetic systems of the automatic nervous system. Furthermore, there is a good deal of evidence to suggest that reducing-augmenting is associated with extraversion-introversion, the second dimension of personality that will be discussed in this book.

REFERENCES

Jensen, A. R.: The Maudsley Personality Inventory. *Acta Psychol, 14*: 14-325, 1958.

Lester, D.: Self-mutilating behavior. *Psychol Bull, 78*: 119-128, 1972.

Lynn, R., and Eysenck, H. J.: Tolerance for pain, extraversion, and neuroticism. *Percept Mot Skills, 12*: 161-162, 1961.

Mumford, J. M., Newton, A. V., and Ley, P.: Personality, pain perception, and pain tolerance. *Br J Psychol, 64*: 105-107, 1973.

Petrie, A.: *Individuality in pain and suffering.* Chicago, University of Chicago Press, 1967.

Silverman, J.: Scanning-control mechanism and "cognitive filtering" in paranoid and nonparanoid schizophrenics. *J Consult Psychol, 28*: 385-393, 1964a.

Silverman, J.: Perceptual control of stimulus intensity in paranoid and nonparanoid schizophrenics. *J Nerv Ment Dis, 139*: 545-549, 1964b.

Simmel, M.: Phantoms in patients with leprosy and in elderly digital amputees. *Am J Psycho, 69*: 529-545, 1956.

Spilker, B., and Callaway, E.: Effects of drugs on "augmenting-reducing" in average visual evoked responses in man. *Psychopharmacol, 15*: 116-124, 1969.

Sweeney, D. R.: Pain reactivity and kinesthetic after effect. *Percept Mot Skills, 22*: 763-769, 1966.

CHAPTER 4 EXTRAVERTS AND INTROVERTS

EYSENCK (1957) has proposed a theory of personality that is based on four, relatively independent, dimensions of personality: intelligence, psychoticism, neuroticism, and introversion-extraversion. The dimension that is relevant for the present theory is that of extraversion-introversion.

Eysenck adopted the notions of Pavlov (1927) and Hull (1943) on excitation and inhibition in the functioning of the central nervous system. Eysenck proposed that the physiological basis for the personality dimension of introversion-extraversion was neural inhibition. He proposed that any response builds up inhibition in the central nervous system, a kind of neural fatigue or refractory period. The inhibition is of the transmission of neural impulses caused by prior-transmitted impulses. Eysenck proposed that individuals differ in the extent to which they build up inhibition. Relatively speaking, some people can be said to have refractory central nervous systems while others have facilitory central nervous systems.

More specifically, Eysenck proposed that introverts were individuals in whom reactive inhibition develops slowly, weak reactive inhibition is generated, reactive inhibition dissipates quickly, excitatory potentials are generated quickly, and excitatory potentials so generated are strong. In contrast, extraverts were seen as individuals in whom reactive inhibition develops quickly, strong reactive inhibition is generated, reactive inhibition dissipates slowly, excitatory potentials are generated slowly, and excitatory potentials so generated are relatively weak.

As Brody (1972) has noted, the critical differentiating factor between introverts and extraverts can be conceptualized as the ratio of inhibition to excitation in the central nervous system of the individuals.

In a more recent statement of his theory, Eysenck (1967) has attempted to relate introversion-extraversion to differences in the threshold of arousal of the reticular formation. Introverts are assumed to have lower thresholds for arousal of the reticular formation than

[20]

extraverts. Differences in the threshold for activation of the visceral brain, or limbic system, were postulated to underlie the dimension of neuroticism.

Eysenck assumed that arousal of the limbic system could lead to arousal of the reticular formation, but not vice versa. Thus, neuroticism, which is associated with low thresholds for activation of the limbic system, should be associated with introversion, since the easily aroused limbic systems of neurotics will in general increase the arousal level of the reticular formation.

(It might be noticed here that Routtenberg [1968], in a thorough review of these two arousal systems, concluded that they were mutually inhibitory and that central nervous system functioning was in part determined by the dynamic balance between the two systems. Routtenberg felt that the reticular formation was primarily concerned with the drive behind and the organization of behavior, whereas the limbic system was primarily concerned with incentive and reward. Routtenberg suggested that the limbic system was involved more in the basic vegetative functions, such as digestion, defecation, temperature control, *ph* control, and so on. The reticular formation appeared to be more involved with sustained [tonic] arousal. It is almost as if the limbic system is more concerned with parasympathetic functioning while the reticular formation is more concerned with sympathetic functioning.)

Eysenck made a number of deductions from his propositions about the differences in the central nervous system of introverts and extraverts: (1) extraverts should perform worse at classical conditioning tasks; (2) extraverts should perform worse at motor performance tasks, such as a finger-tapping task; (3) extraverts should perform worse at vigilance tasks; (4) extraverts should be more susceptible to audioanalgesia; and (5) extraverts should be able to tolerate sensory deprivation less well than introverts. The extravert has been characterized by Eysenck as having a stimulus hunger, while the introvert shows stimulus avoidance.

It should be noted that Eysenck's ideas have stimulated a great deal of research and a great deal of controversy. It is not appropriate here to review this material in detail. It does, however, seem reasonable to conclude that Eysenck's deduction have received a good deal of empirical support.

For example, Brody (1972) has reviewed recent work on the performance of extraverts and introverts at classical conditioning tasks, and found that the results lend only partial support to Eysenck's ideas. Extraverts condition less well than introverts in general only if partial reinforcement schedules are employed, when the UCS intensity is low, when the CS-UCS interval is short, and where anxiety in the experimental situation is low.

Some data to support the physiological differences proposed by Eysenck to account for the behavioral differences between introverts and extraverts come from studies on the sedation threshold, the amount of sedative required to depress cortical arousal. Work by Shagass (Shagass and Jones, 1958) has indicated that extraverts needed less sedative than introverts, although Shagass has usually compared hysterics with other kinds of neurotics and so his studies support Eysenck's theory only if we grant that hysterics are more extraverted than other kinds of neurotics (see below).

Claridge and Herrington (1960) used behavioral rather than physiological measures of sedation and essentially confirmed Shagass's results. However, as Brody (1972) has pointed out, the results for hysterics and other kinds of neurotics do not always parallel the results obtained from comparisons of extraverts and introverts when this personality dimension is measured by a paper-and-pencil personality inventory.

Eysenck has proposed that the process of socialization depends upon the classical conditioning of fear responses, which then facilitates the learning of avoidance responses (avoidance of acts of wrong-doing) by instrumental conditioning. The delinquent is one who has failed to become adequately socialized (that is, learn the avoidance rules of the society), and Eysenck deduced that delinquents would, therefore, be extraverts. Eysenck has produced data to indicate that indeed delinquents obtain higher than average extraversion scores and perform in a way similar to the way that extraverts perform tasks involving perceptual-motor performance and learning tasks.

Eysenck also proposed that patients with hysterical neuroses are neurotic extraverts whereas obsessive-compulsive neurotics, phobics, and anxiety neurotics (all of whom Eysenck called "dysthymics") were neurotic introverts. Again, a good deal of data appears to support this proposition (see Chapter 13, Templer and Lester).

Eysenck noted that brain-damaged patients often behaved like delinquents and he concluded that brain-damaged patients were characterized by increased inhibition in their central nervous systems. Taking all of these ideas into account, it appears that there is a good deal of overlap between Eysenck's dimension of extraversion-introversion and Petrie's dimension of reducing-augmenting (see Chapter 3). Reducers appear to be similar to extraverts while augmenters appear to be similiar to introverts. It is plausible to propose, therefore, that extraverts have sympathetic predominance in their autonomic nervous systems (that is, they are S-types) while introverts have parasympathetic predominance (that is, they are P-types). There is, as yet, little direct data bearing on the functioning of the autonomic nervous system of extraverts and introverts, but the connection between extraversion-introversion and autonomic nervous system balance seems a reasonable one to make.

THE UNIDIMENSIONALITY OF INTROVERSION-EXTRAVERSION

Carrigan (1960) has examined a number of studies on the dimension of extraversion-introversion in order to explore whether the dimension is unidimensional. Her review led her to conclude that the dimension was not unidimensional. For example, data analyzed by Mann (1958) from the extraversion-introversion measures obtained from the personality inventories derived by Guilford and by Cattell led him to conclude that there were (at least) two relatively distinct dimensions. Mann called these social extraversion (which he felt corresponded to the American conception of extraversion, with its emphasis on sociability and ease in interpersonal relations) and lack of self-control (which corresponds to the European conception of extraversion with its emphasis on impulsiveness and weak superego controls).

Mann's analysis is particularly appropriate for the present theory, for the two dimensions of extraversion correspond well with the two types of sympathetic reactions that will be described in Chapters 8 and 9. To anticipate a little, social extraversion seems to be related to an anger-in/anxiety response to stress, an adrenalin response to stress (Funkenstein, 1955), and to Sheldon's (1942) endomorphic type. The lack of self-control dimension seems to be related to an anger-out response to stress, a noradrenalin response to stress, and to Sheldon's mesomorphic type.

A MODIFICATION OF EYSENCK'S THEORY

Gray (1971) has proposed a modification of Eysenck's theory that is of interest here. Whereas Eysenck explains the poorer conditioning of the fear responses of extraverts as due to their general impairment at conditioning, Gray has proposed that the impairment is a narrower one; an insensitivity to punishment and the threat of punishment.

Gray has argued that his hypothesis of a difference in the ability to fear between extraverts and introverts can explain (1) the presence of a subjective feeling of fear in the introverted neurotic and its absence in the extraverted neurotic, (2) the development of overt avoidance behavior in the introverted neurotic (phobias and obsessions) and the failure to develop these in the extraverted neurotic, (3) psychopathic behavior, (4) the impulsive acting of the extravert, which arises because his behavior is more determined by potential rewards and he is less likely to avoid the impulsive actions in the face of prospective punishment, and (5) the liking of the extravert for other people, since they dispense the rewards he likes, while the potential punishments that they might dispense do not concern him. This last point is related to the optimism of extraverts, for extraverts will be less sensitive to prospective punishments.

Gray has proposed a mechanistic model for the operation of rewards and punishments and he has also attempted to localize the parts of his mechanism in the central nervous system. The punishment mechanism is located, according to Gray, in the medial frontal cortex, the medial septal nuclei, and the hippocampus. This allows Gray to predict that frontal lobotomy or leucotomy will make people extraverted because it will interefere with their attending to punishing stimuli. Gray noted that Sodium Amytal® (a sedative) has as one of its chief points of action the septal-hippocampal region. Thus, he predicted that the extravert, with his reduced sensitivity to punishment, probably has an impairment in his septal-hippocampal region and would require less sedative in order to become sedated. The study by Shagass and Jones (1958) mentioned above confirmed this prediction.

Gray reconceptualized neuroticism as based on increased sensitivity to reinforcers in general, whereas extraversion/introversion is based upon the relative sensitivity to rewards versus punishments. Gray predicted that susceptibility to fear, frustration, and anxiety should increase as one moves from stable extraversion to neurotic introversion. Gray hypothesized that manifest anxiety constitutes such a dimension.

As one final comment on Gray's ideas, it is of interest to note that Gray sees depression as a reaction to a loss of an important source of reward. This leads to frustration and is a punishment in Gray's model. Thus, introverts (with their increased sensitivity to punishments relative to rewards) should suffer most from loss. Thus, Gray divides dysthymics into two kinds: (1) those suffering from a high level of fear (phobics, anxiety states, and obsessionals), and (2) those suffering from a high level of frustration (those with reactive depression).

Comment

The dimension of extraversion-introversion seems to be closely related from a conceptual point of view with the dimension of reducing-augmenting. Although there is little direct evidence to link the dimension of extraversion-introversion to the balance of the autonomic nervous system, such a link seems reasonable, and, by association with the dimension of reducing-augmenting, seems quite likely.

REFERENCES

Brody, N.: *Personality.* New York, Academic Press, 1972.

Carrigan, P. M.: Extraversion-introversion as a dimension of personality. *Psychol Bull, 57*: 329-360, 1960.

Claridge, G. W., and Herrington, R. N.: Sedation threshold, personality and the theory of neurosis. *J Ment Sci, 106*:1568-1583, 1960.

Eysenck, H. J.: *The Dynamics Of Anxiety And Hysteria.* London, Routledge and Kegan Paul, 1957.

Eysenck, H. J.: *The Biological Basis Of Personality.* Springfield, Charles C Thomas, 1967.

Funkenstein, D.: The physiology of fear and anger. *Sci Am, 192(5)*:74-80, 1955.

Gray, J.: *The Psychology Of Fear And Stress.* New York, McGraw-Hill, 1971.

Hull, C. L.: *Principles Of Behavior.* New York, Appleton-Century-Crofts, 1943.

Mann, R. D.: The relationship between personality characteristics and individual performance in small groups. Ph.D. thesis, University of Michigan, 1958.

Pavlov, I. P.: *Conditioned Reflexes.* London, Oxford University Press, 1927.

Routtenberg, A.: The two-arousal hypothesis. *Psychol Rev, 75:* 51-80, 1968.

Shagass, C., and Jones, A. L.: A neurophysiological test for psychiatric diagnosis. *Am J Psychiatr, 114:* 1002-1009, 1958.

Sheldon, W. H.: *The Varieties Of Temperament.* New York, Harper, 1942.

Templer, D. I., and Lester, D.: *The Conversion disorders.* In press.

CHAPTER 5 REPRESSORS AND SENSITIZERS

B YRNE (1964) has developed the ideas of previous investigators regarding the dimension of personality labelled as repressing-sensitizing. Repressing involves avoidance of anxiety-arousing stimuli and their consequences. The defense mechanisms involved in repressing include repression, denial, and rationalization. Sensitizing involves attempts to reduce anxiety by approaching and controlling the anxiety-arousing stimuli and their consequences. The defense mechanisms involved in sensitizing include intellectualization, obsessive behaviors, and ruminative worrying.

In order to better assess this dimension of personality, Byrne (1961) derived a scale from the MMPI that has proved reasonably valid for categorizing people on this dimension of personality. In a typical study, Lazarus and Alfert (1964) showed students an anxiety-provoking film or a neutral film. Students classified as repressors indicated less verbal anxiety and less depression in response to the stressful film than did the sensitizers, but their autonomic reactivity to the stressful film was greater. Although this finding has been replicated many times (e.g. Scarpetti, 1973), occasional failures to replicate the basic finding have been reported (e.g. Lewinsohn et al., 1972).

In a variety of studies correlating repressing-sensitizing with other personality variables, sensitizers have been reported to be introverted on the Myers-Briggs Type Indicator, to be socially introverted, depressed, cycloid, and low in rhathymia (or carefreeness) on Guilford's STDCR Inventory, and to be depressed, anxious, and socially introverted on the MMPI (Byrne, 1964). On the California Psychological Inventory, sensitizers have been found to be apathetic, leisurely, passive, submissive, and detached while repressors have been found to be active, alert, competitive, energetic, and sociable. Repressors appear to be overcontrolled on the MMPI scale of over control (Megargee and Mendelsohn, 1964). It has also been reported that alcoholics are sensitizers.

[27]

Many investigators see the dimension of repressing-sensitizing as similar to that of extraversion-introversion and to optimism-pessimism (e.g. Gray, 1971). Some of the results mentioned earlier confirm this hypothesis, but again there are some failures to find such an association (e.g. Shriberg, 1972). Merbaum and Badia (1967) found that sensitizers tolerated significantly less electric shock than did repressors, which allows us to conclude that repressors may be reducers while sensitizers may be augmenters.

Comment

The data reviewed above appear to be consistent with the notion that sensitizers are P-type individuals whereas repressors are S-type individuals. The data suggest an association between repressing and high autonomic reactivity, tolerance for pain (reducing), and extraversion. No studies have yet been reported directly relating repressing-sensitizing to the balance of the autonomic system, and so the conclusion rests on only indirect evidence.

REFERENCES

Byrne, D.: The repression-sensitization scale. *J Pers, 29*: 334-349, 1961.

Byrne, D.: Repression-sensitization as a dimension of personality. In Maher, B. (Ed.): *Progress In Experimental Personality Research.* New York, Academic, 1964, pp. 169-220.

Gray, J.: *The Psychlogy Of Fear And Stress.* New York, McGraw-Hill, 1971.

Lazarus, R., and Alfert, E.: The short circuiting of threat by experimentally altering cognitive appraisal. *J Abnorm Soc Psychol, 69*: 195-205, 1964.

Lewinsohn, P. M., Bergquist, W. H., and Brelje, T.: The repression-sensitization dimension and emotional response to stimuli. *Psychol Rep, 31*: 707-716, 1972.

Megargee, E. I., and Mendelsohn, G.: A cross-validation of twelve MMPI indices of hostility and control. *J Abnorm Soc Psychol, 65*: 431-438, 1962.

Merbaum, M., and Badia, P.: Tolerance of repressors and sensitizers to noxious stimulation. *J Abnorm Psychol, 72*: 349-353, 1967.

Scarpetti, W. L.: The repression-sensitization dimension to impending painful stimulation. *J Consult Clin Psychol, 40*: 377-382, 1973.

Shriberg, L. D.: Intercorrelations among repression-sensitization, extraversion, neuroticism, social desirability, and locus of control. *Psychol Rep, 31*: 925-926, 1972.

CHAPTER 6   FIELD-DEPENDENCE AND FIELD-INDEPENDENCE

WITKIN (1965; Witkin *et al.*, 1954) introduced the notion of a style of behaving based upon the individual's reaction to contextual cues. In one of the tests that assess this response style, the individual is seated in a vertical chair in a dark room. In front of him is a rectangle that is luminous, tilted approximately 45 degrees from the true vertical. In the center of the frame is a luminous rod which the individual has to set to the true vertical. Individuals who are able to ignore the contextual cues from the frame and who set the rod almost vertical are said to be *field independent,* whereas individuals whose setting of the rod is greatly affected by the frame are said to be *field dependent.*

In another test of this behavior, the body-adjustment test, the individual is placed in a room which can be tilted and in which the chair of the individual can be tilted independently. The person's task is to set his chair to the true vertical while the room remains tilted. In a third test of this behavior, the embedded figures test (based on Gottschaldt, 1926) a simple figure is hidden in a complex geometrical figure and the person is timed for how long it takes him to identify the location of the simple figure.

Scores on these three tests are positively correlated with each other. Witkin suggested that these three tests involved the ability to overcome an embedding or field context. This ability permits a person to ignore or de-emphasize irrelevant or misleading stimuli in a situation in order to concentrate on those stimuli that are relevant for a correct response.

Witkin adopted the notion of differentiation (or articulation) which is similar to the concepts introduced by Werner and others (see Mehrabian, 1968), and he suggested that people differed in the differentiation of their conceptual systems. The degree of differentiation refers to the complexity of the conceptual system. Witkin proposed that those people who have differentiated systems have specialized sub-

[29]

systems that can function more or less independently of one another. These people can achieve a degree of separation of their psychological behaviors; feeling from perceiving, thinking from acting, and so on. The parts of their perceptual field are perceived as discrete rather than fused with the background. Impulses are channelized and do not spill over from one to another.

A number of variables have been found to be associated with this personality trait (or cognitive style). Witkin noted that psychological development is accompanied by increasing differentiation. Thus, older persons are, up to a point, more field independent than young people. Witkin hypothesized that people who are relatively undifferentiated (that is, who are field dependent) should tend to use relatively primitive defense mechanisms such as repression and denial, whereas relatively differentiated people (that is, who are field independent) will use defense mechanisms like intellectualization. (Witkin proposed this because the defense mechanisms of repression and denial are seen by psychoanalysts as primitive and acting in an undifferentiated manner.) Many of Witkin's studies to test this hypothesis utilized unvalidated projective tests. However, Witkin did report a relationship between field dependence and the inability to recall dreams.

Other studies have shown that field dependent people are more influenced by the responses of others in tests of conformity (such as assessing the amount of movement of the autokinetic effect in a group situation). Minard and Mooney (1969) found that field independent persons were less influenced in their cognitive functioning by their emotional reactions to the stimuli. There is a good deal of data to suggest that field independence is associated with verbal and nonverbal intelligence test scores. Also, males are found to be more field independent than females.

Field independence has been found to be correlated with high rates of reversal in the perception of reversible figures such as the Necker cube and with long spiral after-effects. Field independence is also correlated with better performance on the Stroop Color-Word Test and on a two-point tactile discrimination task. Field dependent people seem to tolerate sensory deprivation less well than field independent people (they have greater autonomic arousal, more hallucinations, more disruption of thought processes, and more discomfort).*

A number of studies have related field dependence and field independence to the personality dimensions considered in previous chapters. Evans (1967) reported that extraverts were field dependent, as did Taft and Coventry (1958). Two points are relevant to this association. First, some investigators have failed to replicate the association (e.g. Du Preez, 1967). Second, Fine and Cohen (1963) reported that extraverts are less accurate in setting a rod to vertical even when there is no frame present. This general inaccuracy of extraverts has not been controlled for in studies of the association between extraversion and field dependence utilizing the rod-and-frame test. (The studies by Evans and by Du Preez used the embedded figures test to measure field dependence, thus avoiding this problem.)

With respect to the association between reducing-augmenting and field dependence-independence, Sweeney and Fine (1965) reported that field independent subjects had a high pain reactivity (and so were augmenters).

These studies are quite consistent from the point of view of the present theory. On the whole, it appears that field dependent people tolerate sensory deprivation less well and have shorter spiral after-effects, which is consistent with their being S-types. Thus, field independent people are P-types.† This is consistent with the studies on two-point tactile discrimination, the sex differences (see Chapter 18), the age differences and the differences in the defense mechanisms used (see Chapter 5).

The conclusion that field dependent people are S-types is consistent with their being extraverts and reducers, whereas field independent people are introverts and augmenters. McGough et al. (1965) have reported that tests of the mobilization of free fatty acids by the body (which is thought to assess sympathetic system predominance) indicate that the level of free fatty acids is higher in field dependent people, which again is consistent with our conclusion.

---

*This summary of research was based primarily upon Witkin (1965), Long (1972), and Silverman, et al. (1967).

†The derivation of the prediction for spiral after-effects and extraversion-introversion is given by Eysenck (1965).

PSYCHOPATHOLOGY

With respect to psychopathology, it has been reported that field dependence is characteristic of patients with ulcers, obese people, asthmatic children, patients with character disorders (that is, generally inadequate personalities unable to manage the ordinary problems of living), patients who somatize their complaints and deny any psychological problems, patients with hysterical character structures, and patients with functional cardiac disorders. Field independence is characteristic of obsessive-compulsive neurotics, hypertensive patients, and ambulatory schizophrenics with a well-developed defensive structure. Psychotics who hallucinate are more likely to be field dependent whereas delusional psychotics are more likely to be field independent. Process schizophrenics seem to be field dependent, whereas reactive schizophrenics seem to be field independent. Alcoholics are found to be field dependent, and this is true when they are drinking and when they are abstaining, when they are drunk and when they are sober, and for long-term drinkers and relatively new drinkers.

The evidence relating to psychopathology will be reviewed in greater detail in Part Four. To summarize the conclusions, it may be noted that the data on obese people fit into the theory and, that the data on schizophrenics fit into the theory if we use Petrie's hypothesis that schizophrenics are born as P-types and act like S-types as a defensive reaction (*see* Chapters 3 and 12). Only the data on alcoholics create some problems for integration (*see* Chapter 10).

FIELD DEPENDENCE-FIELD INDEPENDENCE
AND AROUSAL

A number of studies have reported physiological differences, often in terms of arousal, between those who are field dependent and those who are field independent. However, these studies have not been altogether consistent.

Some studies report that transient increases in arousal lead to increased field independence. Drug-induced arousal has led to increased field independence on the embedded figures test (Callaway, 1959) and white noise has led to increased field independence on the rod-and-frame test (Oltman, 1964). Oltman noted that a large body of literature exists which indicates that, under conditions of arousal, there appears to be a focussing or narrowing of the individual's perceptual field and, hence, a reduction in the amount of environmental stimuli to which he can attend. Oltman argued that this perceptual focussing would cause the individual to attend to particular aspects of the environment (the figure) while ignoring the distracting contextual stimuli (the ground).

In support of this position, a number of studies have shown greater autonomic reactivity to stimuli in field independent people than in field dependent people (for example, Hein *et al.,* 1965). Long (1972) cites the ideas of Broverman *et al.* (1968; *see* Chapter 18) as supporting Oltman's thesis. In fact, the two sets of ideas conflict. Broverman, *et al.* attribute the superior performance of males on the rod-and-frame test (that is, their field independence) as due to the parasympathetic system being predominant in males, whereas the sympathetic system is predominant in females. Thus, Broverman *et al.* see field independence as related to a less dominant sympathetic system. On the other hand, the implication of Oltman's thesis is that autonomic arousal (which usually means sympathetic system arousal) is associated with field independence, the reverse of Broverman's thesis.

Long (1972) also argues that data on age differences in field-independence and field dependence support the arousal hypothesis. Long noted that stable sex differences become noticeable first at about the time of puberty, when hormone levels are undergoing changes. In old age, when hormone levels again undergo change, not only do both males and females become more field dependent, but also the sex difference disappears.

In contrast to the above studies, a number of studies have demonstrated that increased arousal to stress was characteristic of field dependent people. For example, field dependent people seem to respond with greater autonomic arousal to sensory deprivation (Silverman *et al.,* 1961). (This association would obviously be consistent with the thesis proposed by Broverman *et al.* [1968].)

In an attempt to reconcile these conflicting studies, Morf, *et al.* (1971) have suggested that the relationship between autonomic arousal and field-independence and field-dependence was not linear. They suggested that increases in arousal up to a point led to greater field independence, but that further increases in arousal lead to field dependence.

Long (1972) has attempted a different reconciliation. Long has argued that investigators fail to distinguish between two kinds of physiological measures. Some use measures of autonomic arousal (such as the amplitude or length of the galvanic skin response) while others use measures such as the frequency of the galvanic skin response or the number of EEG responses, which Long viewed as measures of autonomic nervous system stability (Lacey, 1967). Long concluded that field dependent people are more labile in the functioning of their autonomic nervous systems, but that they function at a lower level of autonomic arousal than field independent people. Thus, for Long, field independent people have greater sympathetic predominance.

Wenger (1966) has conducted a number of studies using physiological measures to assess autonomic nervous system balance. A number of measures (such as salivary output, dermographia persistence, palmar conductance, volar conductance, diastolic blood pressure, heart period, and respiration period) are highly intercorrelated and are believed by Wenger to assess whether the sympathetic or the parasympathetic system is predominant. Long (1972) noted that diagnostic groups found by Wenger to have sympathetic predominance have been found to be field independent on Witkin's tests of field independence (for example, paranoid schizophrenics). On the other hand, diagnostic groups found by Wenger to have parasympathetic predominance have been found to be field dependent (for example, peptic ulcer patients and asthmatic patients). Long noted that no studies have been conducted as yet that directly correlate Wenger's tests of autonomic balance and Witkin's measures of field-independence and field dependence, but Long predicted that the two dimensions will be found to be closely related.

FINE'S THEORY

Fine (1972) has proposed a theory concerning the association between field dependence and extraversion that does not concur with the ideas proposed in this chapter, but which deserves mention. Fine noted that extraversion and field dependence are often seen as related (e.g. Eysenck, 1967). Fine noted, for example, that his studies showed that field dependent people were more tolerant of pain but that extraverts and introverts did not differ in their pain tolerance. Fine examined the implications of the notion that field-dependence and extraversion were independent dimensions of personality. Fine then considered the special subgroup of people who were field dependent introverts. Fine noted that field dependent people are intolerant of isolation, have a better memory for human faces, are oriented toward social approval, and are oriented toward others (which sounds to the present author suspiciously like a description of the typical extravert). Thus, the field dependent introvert will have, according to Fine, a need for external stimulation but will also have a built-in inability to get it (since he is an introvert). Fine speculated that this conflict would lead to neuroticism. In a number of analyses of data, Fine found that field dependence was unrelated to extraversion, and that field dependent introverts were the most neurotic subgroup. (It might be noted that in none of the studies that Fine analyzed was field dependence measured by the rod-and-frame test.)

Fine noted that his view of the field dependent introvert was quite similar to the description of the overcontrolled individual described by Megargee (1966).

Comment

I have discussed the issue of the relationship between field-independence and field dependence and the balance in the autonomic nervous system in some detail primarily because the relationship is by no means clear at the present time. Thus, it was important to demonstrate that a large number of investigators are confident that a relationship does exist and that they are currently seeking to define the relationship.

It is clear from this review that, on the whole, the data do presently allow a reliable conclusion to be drawn as to the direction of the association: field dependent people are S-types, whereas field independent people are P-types.

In this regard, it is appropriate to point to one source of possible confusion in these studies. As Lester (1968) has pointed out, many investigators of the rod-and-frame test simply do not know how to use the equipment. The majority of studies using the apparatus do not control for head position, starting position effects, or the effect of instructions. Some investigators do not take control readings. Other investigators do not take into account the direction of the errors made.*

---

*For example, if a subject sets the rod 5° to the left on one trail and 5° to the right on the next, some investigators score this as 10° of error (and thus relatively

As Lester concluded:

> In the opinion of the present author, there may indeed be underlying perceptual and/or personality factors [in performance at the rod-and-frame task], but they will be found only after methodology is improved and implicit information is controlled.

In the light of this trenchant criticism of the research methodology of rod-and-frame studies, it is perhaps not surprising that the results of these studies are not altogether consistent at the present time.

REFERENCES

Broverman, D., Klaiber, E., Kobayashi, Y., and Vogel, W.: Role of activation and inhibition in sex differences in cognitive abilities. *Psychol Rev, 75*: 23-50, 1968.

Callaway, E.: The influence of amobarbital (amylbarbitone) and methamphetamine on the focus of attention. *J Ment Sci, 105*: 382-392, 1959.

Du Preeze, P.: Field dependency and accuracy of comparison of time intervals. *Percept Mot Skills, 24*: 467-472, 1967.

Evans, F. J.: Field dependence and the Maudsley Personality Inventory. *Percept Mot Skills, 24*: 526, 1967.

Eysenck, H. J.: *Fact And Fiction In Psychology.* Baltimore, Penguin, 1965.

Eysenck, H. J.: *The Biological Basis Of Personality.* Springfield, Charles C Thomas, 1967.

Fine, B. J.: Field-dependent introvert and neuroticism. *Psychol Rep, 31*: 939-756, 1972.

Fine, B. J., and Cohen, A.: Internalization ratio, accuracy, and variability of judgments of the vertical. *Percept Mot Skills, 16*: 138, 1963.

Gottschaldt, K.: Uber der Einfluss der Erfahrung auf die Wahrnehmung von Figuren. *Psychol Forsch, 8*: 261-317, 1926.

Hein, P., Cohen, S., and Shmavonian, B. M.: Perceptual mode and Pavlovian typology. In Wortis, J. (Ed.): *Recent Advances In Biological Psychiatry: Volume 7.* New York, Plenum, 1965, pp. 71-78.

Lacey, J. T.: Somatic response patterning and stress. In Appley, M., and Trumbull, R. (Eds.): *Psychological Stress.* New York, Appleton-Century-Crofts, 1967, pp. 14-44.

Lester, G.: The rod-and-frame test. *Percept Mot Skills, 26*: 1307-1314, 1968.

Long, G.: *Field-dependency-independency.* Pensacola, Naval Aerospace Medical Research Laboratory, 1972.

McGough, W. E., Silverman, A. J., and Bogdonoff, M. D.: Patterns of fat mobilization in field dependent and field independent subjects. *Psychosom Med, 27*: 245-256, 1965.

---

field dependent) whereas others score it as 0° (and thus relatively field independent).

Megargee, E.: Undercontrolled and overcontrolled personality types in extreme antisocial aggression. *Psychol Monogr, 80*: #3, 1966.

Mehrabian, A.: *An Analysis Of Personality Theories.* Englewood Cliffs, Prentice-Hall, 1968.

Minard, J. G., and Mooney, W.: Psychological differentiation and perceptual defence. *J Abnorm Psycho, 74*: 131-139, 1969.

Morf, M. E., Kavanaugh, R. D., and McConville, M.: Intratest and sex differences on a portable rod-and-frame test. *Percept Mot Skills, 32*: 727-733, 1971.

Oltman, P. K.: Field dependence and arousal. *Percept Mot Skills, 19*: 441, 1964.

Silverman, A. J., Cohen, S. I., Shmavonian, B. M., and Greenberg, G.: Psychophysiological investigations in sensory deprivation. *Psychosom Med, 23*: 48-62, 1961.

Silverman, A. J., McGough, W. E., and Bogdonoff, M. D.: Perceptual correlates of the physiological response to insulin. *Psychosom Med, 29*: 252-264, 1967.

Sweeney, D. R., and Fine, B. J.: Pain reactivity and field dependence. *Percept Mot Skills, 21*: 757-758, 1965.

Taft, R., and Coventry, J.: Neuroticism, extraversion and the perception of the vertical. *J Abnorm Soc Psychol, 56*: 139-141, 1958.

Wenger, M. A.: Studies of autonomic balance. *Psychophysiology, 2*: 173-186, 1966.

Witkin, H.: Psychological differentiation and forms of pathology. *J Abnorm Psychol, 70*: 317-336, 1965.

Witkin, H., Lewis, H., Hertzman, M., Machover, K., Meissner, P., and Wapner, S.: *Personality Through Perception.* New York, Harper, 1954.

CHAPTER 7 OTHER PERSONALITY TRAITS

THERE ARE MANY other personality traits that would appear to have a possible relationship to the theory proposed in this book, but for which there are too few data with which to adequately test the fit. However, some of these traits are worth noting here briefly.

Anxiety Reactivity

Lykken (unpublished) has devised an activity preference questionnaire in which subjects have to choose between an onerous task and an anxiety-provoking task. Lykken found that psychopaths obtained higher scores than normals for choice of anxiety-provoking tasks. Scores were also correlated with a psychophysical measure of arousal (the two-flash threshold) and with Byrne's repression-sensitization scale. Thus, it would seem possible that thrill-seekers are S-types while thrill avoiders are P-types.

It would also seem likely that other sensation-seeking scales, such as Zuckerman's (Zuckerman and Link, 1968) would be related to sympathetic predominance. Similarly, the classification proposed by Balint (1959) of "philobats" and "ocnophiles" involves thrill-seeking and hence might also be related to autonomic balance.

Cattell's Universal Factors

Cattell (1957) has given single individuals batteries of psychological tests repeatedly so that day-to-day variations in test scores could be identified. Among the factors extracted from these data include three that are relevant to autonomic balance.

Cattell identified three factors which he named adrenergic, parasympathetic and general autonomic metabolic rate. He has described the parasympathetic factor, for example, as loading high on skin resistance, blood sugar levels, serum cholinesterase level, and various test performances indicating unreactiveness, inhibition, and disinclination to become involved. Cattell has argued that this dimension should not be mistaken for fatigue.

It is by no means clear whether Cattell has identified a similar set of factors for cross-sectional studies (giving a large number of people the same tests) as well as for longitudinal studies.

Levelers and Sharpeners

Holzman and Gardner (1959) have identified a cognitive style which they have called leveling-sharpening. A cognitive style is an habitual way of responding to stimuli and making perceptual judgments. Leveling-sharpening refers to the degree of differentiation of memory schema. Levelers tend to minimize differences whereas sharpeners preserve or accentuate differences. This behavior is usually measured by tests of size estimation in which the stimuli are gradually changed in size without telling the subject. The experimenter measures the degree to which the subject notices that change in the stimuli has occurred.

Evidence suggesting that leveling-sharpening might relate to the present theory is scarce, but Holzman and Gardner (1959) found that the cognitive style of leveling was associated with the use of the defense mechanism of repression. They noted that repression was similar to assimilation, since assimilated items lose their identity and hence their availability to consciousness. Brain-damaged people also tend to be levelers. Klein (1951) noted that levelers had more difficulty finding hidden figures embedded in a complex design, and this suggests that levelers are field dependent.

On this scanty evidence, we can guess that levelers are S-types while sharpeners are P-types.

Eye Pigment

With increasing amount of eye pigment, the color of eyes in humans moves from blue to green and hazel, and finally to brown. Eye pigment is genetically determined and, if eye color should be found to be related to personality, it seems reasonable to conclude that personality may have genetic determinants.

In fact, Kent (1956) has reported that blue-eyed people have a lower pulse pressure, a higher pulse rate, a higher respiratory rate, and higher oral temperatures than brown-eyed people. There are also some data to suggest that blue-eyed people are active, outgoing, sociable and extraverted, whereas brown-eyed people are passive, dreamy, and introverted (Lowe, 1969).

It appears possible that blue-eyed people are S-types while brown-eyed people are P-types.

Brain Damage

I noted above that brain-damaged people tend to be levelers and in Chapter 4 it was noted that they tend to be more extraverted. Birch and Steinberg (1962) studied hemiplegic patients and noted reduced galvanic skin responses to stimuli in almost half of the patients. All the patients had a higher threshold for electric shock than normals and all had high blood pressure (both systolic and diastolic) and higher pulse rates. Birch *et al.* (1964) found that under some circumstances, brain-damaged patients underestimated the intensity of tones.

Thus, brain-damaged patients appear to be S-types and this fits in with available data on the effects of sympathetic system activation which suggests that such activation leads to focusing and narrowing of perception (Callaway and Dembo, 1958).

Comment

The range of potential applicability of the theory presented so far is large. Numerous authors have proposed concepts and constructs that could be related to the parasympathetic-sympathetic balance of the autonomic nervous system. In addition, many authors have involved the autonomic nervous system in their ideas without developing this involvement to any great extent. For example, Richter (1959) noted that domestication in rats has been accompanied by a reduction in the size of the adrenal gland. This, if true, might have led to a shift in the balance of the autonomic system from sympathetic predominance to parasympathetic predominance. Richter has speculated upon the effects of civilization in man based upon his work with wild and domesticated rats.

One final variable that we might mention is that of age. A number of references to variation in the personality traits discussed here with age have been made in this book: field-dependence (Chapter 6), endomorphy (Chapter 9), and repression-sensitization (Chapter 19). The variation of personality with age is complex, since in all probability the variation is not linear from childhood to adolescence, to adulthood, and to old age. However, autonomic balance and associated personality traits do appear to vary with age.

Clearly, the potential applications of the theory are large. However, it is now time to elaborate the theory a little further. The aim is to transform the theory from a two category theory to a three category theory, and to do this I will discuss the work of Funkenstein on sympathetic system activation.

REFERENCES

Balint, M.: *Thrills And Regressions.* New York, International Universities Press, 1959.

Birch, H., and Steinberg, R.: Changes in autonomic functioning in hemiplegia. *Arch Phys Med, 43*: 518-524, 1962.

Birch, H., Belmont, I., and Karp, E.: Excitation-inhibition balance in brain-damaged patients. *J Nerv Ment Dis, 139*: 537-544, 1964.

Callaway, E., and Dembo, D.: Narrowed attention. *Arch Neurol Psychiatr, 79*: 74-90, 1958.

Cattell, R. B.: *Personality And Motivation Structure And Measurement.* New York, World, 1957.

Holzman, P., and Gardner, R.: Leveling and repression. *J Abnorm Soc Psychol, 59*: 151-155, 1959.

Kent, I.: Human iris pigment. *Canad Psychiatr Assoc J, 1*: 99-104, 1956.

Klein, G.: The personal world through perception. In Blake, R. R., and Ramsey, G. V. (Eds.): *Perception.* New York, Ronald, 1951, pp. 328-355.

Lowe, G. R.: Eye colour and personality. *Mankind Q, 9*: 178-187, 1969.

Lykken, D.: Instructions for experimental users of the "Activity Preference Questionnaire." Unpublished.

Richter, C.: Rats, man and the welfare state. *Am Psychol, 14*: 18-28, 1959.

Zuckerman, M., and Link, K.: Construct validity for the sensation-seeking scale. *J Consult Clin Psychol, 32*: 420-426, 1968.

PART THREE　　**THREE TRAIT THEORIES**

CHAPTER 8 ANGER-IN AND ANGER-OUT

So far we have relied on a dichotomous classification of autonomic nervous system functioning and we have related this dichotomy to various personality traits. The work of Funkenstein and his associates enables us to extend our dichotomy and propose a tripartite categorization.

Funkenstein *et al.* (1954) subjected college students to stress and noted that the three most common reactions reported were depression (anger-in), rage (anger-out), and anxiety. The groups did not differ in the reaction of their blood pressure to stress, but their pulse rates differed significantly. The pulse rates of the anger-out group differed significantly from the pulse rates of the anger-in group and the anxiety group. These latter two groups were very similar in their physiological response to stress.

Funkenstein *et al.* (1952) injected mecholyl into psychiatric patients and found that for those diagnosed as manic-depressive or as involutional melancholics the blood pressure dropped and stayed low. For those diagnosed as schizophrenic, the blood pressure dropped but rose quickly back to its customary level. When patients who showed the different physiological patterns of response to mecholyl injections were evaluated by psychiatrists, those showing a marked and persistent drop in blood pressure were judged depressed or frightened, while those showing a small transient response were judged to be angry (and often paranoid).

When college students awaiting the results of their applications for internships were studied, again those who were angry showed a small drop in blood pressure after injections of mecholyl, whereas those who were depressed and anxious showed a marked drop.

Funkenstein (1955) argued that when the blood pressure was elevated by noradrenalin, mecholyl caused a small drop in blood pressure. Thus, an anger-out reaction to stress was postulated to be associated with noradrenalin secreation (in my terminology S type, subtype N). On the other, when blood pressure was elevated by adrenalin, mecholyl injections caused a large drop in blood pressure. Thus, anger-in and anxiety responses to stress were postulated to be associated with secretion of adrenalin (in my terminology S type, subtype A). These ideas were supported by studies in which normal college students were injected with adrenalin or noradrenalin, and then mecholyl was injected and the reactions of the students' blood pressure to the injections monitored.

The associations between emotional response and physiological response proposed by Funkenstein were also tested by inducing emotional responses in the same students (at different times) and observing the kind of physiological reactions that accompanied the different emotional reactions.

Funkenstein noted how studies on wild animals confirmed his general ideas. Animals which are aggressive in the wild had high levels of noradrenalin secretion whereas social and timid animals had high levels of adrenalin secretion. Funkenstein also noted that, with advancing age in humans, there was a shift from noradrenalin predominance to adrenalin predominance in the sympathetic system.

Since the appearance of Funkenstein's research, there has been some criticism of its validity (e.g. Beck, 1967), but on the whole his basic ideas seem to be generally accepted (Averill, 1968; Fehr and Stern, 1970). If we grant his ideas a measure of validity, then his ideas have great import for the thesis presented in this book, since they allow the simple dichotomy that I have used hitherto (S-type and P-type) to be extended into a tripartite categorization (P-type, S-type subtype A, and S-type subtype N). This allows theories of personality that employ tripartite categorizations to be incorporated into the thesis proposed in this book. To illustrate this, I will examine the theory of personality proposed by Sheldon (1942).

REFERENCES

Averill, J., and Opton, E.: Psychophysiological assessment. In McReynolds, P. (Ed.): *Advances In Psychological Assessment, Vol. I.* Palo Alto, Science and Behavior Book, 1968, pp. 265-288.

Beck, A. T.: *Depression.* New York, Hoeber, 1967.

Fehr, F., and Stern, J.: Peripheral physiological variables and emotion. *Psychol Bull, 74:* 411-424, 1970.

Funkenstein, D. H.: The physiology of fear and anger. *Sci Am, 192(5):* 74-80, 1955.

Funkenstein, D., Greenblatt, M., and Solomon, H.: Nor-epinephrine like and epinephrine like substances in psychotic and neurotic patients. *Am J Psychiatr, 108*: 652-662, 1952.

Funkenstein, D., King, S., and Drolette, M.: The direction of anger during laboratory stress-inducing situation. *Psychosom Med, 16*: 404-413, 1954.

Sheldon, W. H.: *The Varieties Of Temperament.* New York, Harper, 1942.

CHAPTER 9

SHELDON'S CONSTITUTIONAL THEORY OF PERSONALITY*

IT IS COMMONLY believed that physical characteristics of people tell us something about their personalities and a number of psychologists have pursued this idea. Sheldon (1942) has argued that the association between physique and temperament or personality is more than conicidental: the physique causes the personality. To put it more accurately, there exists a hypothetical biological structure (which Sheldon called the morphogenotype) which underlies the external, observable physique (phenotype). This morphogenotype not only determines physique but also molds behavior.

To test the association between physique and personality, Sheldon adopted the older typology of Kretschmer (1925) who classified people as asthenics, athletics, and pyknics. Sheldon identified three primary components of physique (somatotypes or phenotypes) that are approximate measures of the morphogenotypes.

Endomorphy involves softness and a spherical appearance. Bone and muscle are underdeveloped and the surface/mass ratio is low. The endomorph has a low center of gravity, floats high in the water, and is, in short, fat. The term endomorph comes from the fact that the viscera of the digestive system develop from the endodermal embryonic layer.

Mesomorphy involves a hard rectangular body with a high predominance of bone and muscle. The mesomorph's body is strong, tough, resistant to injury, and can cope with strenuous and exacting exercise. The dominant parts of this physique derive from the mesodermal embryonic layer: hence the term.

The *ectomorph* is linear and fragile. He has a flat chest and delicate body. He is usually thin and lightly muscled. He has a high surface/mass ratio. He also has the largest brain and central nervous system,

---

*This chapter draws heavily from Hall and Lindzey's (1970) description of Sheldon's theory.

[48]

given his size. The term comes from the fact that Sheldon believed that his physique is made up most from tissues that derive from the ectodermal embryonic layer.

Sheldon derived a method for measuring quantitively the degree of each of the somatotypes that the body of a particular individual has. Thus, each person can be described as a three digit number; for example, a person described as (6,4,2) is relatively high in endomorphy, average in mesomorphy, and low in ectomorphy, if the measures for each dimension of the somatotype ranges from 1 to 7.

To describe personality, Sheldon used a tripartite classification system. The *viscerotonic* is dependent, calm, affable, warm, sociable, soft-tempered, and affectionate. The *somatotonic* is dominant, cheerful, energetic, competitive, assertive, and hot-tempered. The *cerebrotonic* is anxious, shy, introspective, sensitive, withdrawn, and precise.

Much of the research that has stemmed from Sheldon's theory has focussed on the extent of the correlations between the dimensions of physique and the dimensions of personality. Although the correlations are often low, endomorphy is associated with most viscerotonia, mesomorphy with somatotonia, and ectomorphy with cerebrotonia.

Hall and Lindzey (1970) have discussed possible mediators of the physique/personality association, and they suggested three possibilities. It may be that environmental influences and/or biological factors lead both to a particular physique and to a particular personality. A second alternative is that the relation between physique and personality is determined by social expectations. If a society expects fat people to be jovial, then well-socialized fat people will act jovial. A third alternative is that biological factors and/or environmental influences make people with particular physiques develop particular personalities. Sheldon himself would have preferred alternatives which placed the biological factors as causes of the personality.

Several correlates of the dimensions of physique have been noted. Sheldon claimed that endomorphy was associated with manic-depressive tendencies, mesomorphy with paranoid tendencies, and ectomorphy with hebephrenic tendencies. Many investigators have found that delinquents are above average in mesomorphy and slightly above average in endomorphy (Sheldon, 1942; Glueck and Glueck, 1950; Cortes and Gatti, 1970). Sheldon (1954) extended his studies to females and found that female physiques were more endomorphic than male physiques. Cortes and Gatti (1970) found that mesomorphy correlated significantly with the male values of the Edwards Personal Preference Schedule (Edwards, 1959) and with a high need to achieve. Witkin (1965) noted that obese people were field dependent. Eysenck (1964) noted that both endomorphs and mesomorphs are extraverted; the difference seems to lie in that the endomorph shows the sociability side of extraversion whereas the mesomorph shows the impulsive side of extraversion. Rees (1968) reported that dysthymics were ectomorphs whereas hysterics were endomorphs. Patients with ulcers and patients suffering from asthma appeared to have a wide variety of physiques. Conrad (1963) has noted that, if size is controlled for, then humans become less endomorphic and more ectomorphic as they grow older, until young adulthood is reached. Thereafter, endomorphic tendencies begin to become more prominent.

How do Sheldon's types fit into the schema proposed in this book? The ectomorph resembles quite closely the parasympathetic type (P-type). He is introverted and has schizoid tendencies. The endomorph and mesomorph both resemble the sympathetic type (S-type). Both are extroverts, for example. They differ in the way that the anger-out and the anger-in people described in the previous chapter differ. The endomorphs resemble the adrenalin subtype whereas the mesomorph resembles the noradrenalin subtype. This is most clearly indicated by the fact that the mesomorph is aggressive, assertive and competitive (anger-out) while the endomorph is more prone to depression (anger-in). Mesomorphs are prone to paranoid schizophrenia and delinquency, whereas endomorphs are prone to manic-depressive disorders.

Comment

It can be seen, therefore, that a typology that utilizes three categories can easily be fitted into the theory proposed in this book. Although the theory is based upon a dichotomy, the existence of two kinds of S-types (adrenalin and noradrenalin) provides the basis for tripartite classifications. (Luckily, psychologists rarely propose more complex classificatory schemes.) The similarities between mesomorphy and endomorphy (in that both physiques are related to extraversion and sympathetic system predominance) provides an explanation for why some investigators feel that Sheldon's three physiques are collapsible down to two physiques (for example, Humphreys, 1957). A two-system division of physique combines the physiques of mesomorphy and endomorphy into one category.

REFERENCES

Conrad, K.: *Der Constitutionstypus.* Berlin, Springer, 1963.

Cortes, J., and Gatti, F.: Physique and propensity. *Psychol Today, 4*(5): 42-44, 82-84, 1970.

Edwards, A. L.: *Edwards Personal Preference Schedule.* New York, Psychological Corporation, 1959.

Eysenck, H. J.: *Crime And Personality.* Boston, Houghton-Mifflin, 1964.

Glueck, S., and Glueck, E.: *Unraveling Juvenile Delinquency.* New York, Commonwealth Fund, 1950.

Hall, C. S., and Lindzey, G.: *Theories Of Personality.* New York, Wiley, 1970.

Humphreys, L. G.: Characteristics of type concepts with special reference to Sheldon's typology. *Psychol Bull, 54:* 218-228, 1957.

Kretschmer, E.: *Physique And Character.* New York, Harcourt, 1925.

Rees, L.: Constitutional psychology. In Sills, D. L. (Ed.): *International Encyclopedia Of The Social Sciences, Vol. 13.* New York, Macmillan, 1968, pp. 66-76.

Sheldon, W. H.: *The Varieties Of Temperament.* New York, Harper, 1942.

Sheldon, W. H.: *Atlas Of Men.* New York, Harper, 1954.

Witkin, H.: Psychological differentiation and forms of pathology. *J Abnorm Psychol, 70:* 317-336, 1965.

PART FOUR **PSYCHOPATHOLOGY**

CHAPTER 10 ALCOHOLICS

ALTHOUGH REFERENCES have been made to alcoholism in earlier chapters, it is by no means easy to fit alcoholics into the theory proposed in this book. There are several issues involved, the first of which concerns the effects of alcohol on people.

The work of Petrie (Chapter 3) suggested that alcohol made augmenters act as if they were reducers, but alcohol had little effect on reducers. The work of Eysenck (Chapter 4) suggested that alcohol made introverts act as if they were extraverts (by inhibiting the central nervous system, according to Eysenck's theory). Thus, the data from these two sources suggests that alcohol makes those who are P-types act as if they were S-types. Hobson (1966) reported that alcohol impairs performance at a classical conditioning task, which supports the proposed effect of alcohol.

When we consider alcoholics, however, we have to rule out the effects of their alcoholic intake from their personality. Alcohol may make people act like S-types, but this does not mean that alcoholics were S-types before they began ingesting alcohol. Petrie (1967) reported that alcoholics were augmenters (and thus P-types), and she reported data that indicated that alcoholics scored high in introversion on personality tests. Thus, this evidence indicates that alcoholics are P-types, a state that cannot be attributed to the effects of alcohol, which would make them act like reducers and extraverts (or S-types).

A number of studies support this classification of alcoholics. Hobson (1971) reported that alcoholics perform better than normals on classical conditioning tasks and Chess et al. (1971) reported that alcoholics are sensitizers and score higher on the Taylor Manifest Anxiety Scale (which appears to tap neurotic introversion—see Chapter 4). As a result of treatment the alcoholics became more repressing and less anxious. Many investigators see alcoholism as an escape from tension, anxiety, or a painful life situation (Zax and Cowen, 1972). For example, Masserman et al. (1944) found that cats turned to alcohol as a relief from conflict-caused stress, and Horton (1943)

[55]

found that the use of alcohol was greater in societies with greater subsistence hazards.

However, it is consistently reported that alcoholics are field dependent (Witkin 1965; Chess *et al.*, 1971). This finding is inconsistent with the proposed classification of alcoholics as P-types, if our classification of field dependence-independence (see Chapter 6) is correct. Furthermore, Chess *et al.* found no differences in the heart rate or skin resistance of alcoholics, anxiety neurotics, and normals. Coleman (1972) reported that alcoholics commonly have symptoms of depression and antisocial behavior, but these symptoms probably appear when under the influence of alcohol (which would make the individuals act like S-types, see above).

(In this connection, mention should be made of Fine's [1972] proposal that extraversion and field dependence are independent dimensions—see Chapter 6. For Fine, neurotics are field dependent introverts. Perhaps alcoholics are field independent introverts.)

Although presumably, alcoholics are administered psychological tests when "dried-out," the vast quantities of alcohol that they have consumed in the past may have caused long-term physiological changes in their bodies. Thus, we do not know what the functioning (both psychological and psysiological) of alcoholics was prior to the beginning of their ingestion of their first drink. (For example, in Chapter 12, it will be argued that, although schizophrenics act as if they are reducers or S-types, they were born as extreme augmenters or P-types. Their present reducing behavior is a defense against sensory bombardment and overstimulation. Thus, present functioning may differ considerably from functioning in infancy.)

It is interesting to note that endocrine theories of alcoholism have been proposed. It has been suggested, for example, that alcohol ingestion could cause hyperactivity of the pituitary gland, eventual exhaustion of the adrenal cortex, and a consequent breakdown in the functions regulated by the adrenal hormones. Recent research in animals and man indicates that alcohol stimulates the adrenal cortex, resulting in the release of its hormones (NIMH, 1971). However, Zarrow *et al.* (1960) found that removal of the adrenal gland had no effect on alcohol intake in rats. It should be noted that this endocrine theory does not propose a cause of alcoholism, but rather describes the result of excessive alcohol intake. However, it is easy to modify the theory to propose an inherited or congenital insufficiency of the adrenal cortex, or at least an inherited or congenital sensitivity to the effects of alcohol.

Comment

It appears that alcoholics can be fitted tentatively into the present theory of personality as P-types. However, not all of the data is consistent with this classification (notably, the data on field dependence-independence) and there must remain some doubt as to the premorbid state of alcoholics.

REFERENCES

Chess, S. B., Neuringer, C., and Goldstein, C.: Arousal and field dependency. *J Gen Psychol, 85*: 93-102, 1971.
Coleman, J. C.: *Abnormal Psychology and Modern Life.* Glenview, Scott Foresman, 1972.
Fine, B. J.: Field-dependent introvert and neuroticism. *Psychol Rep, 31*: 939-956, 1972.
Hobson, G. N.: Ethanol and conditioning. *Q J Stud Alc, 27*: 612-619, 1966.
Hobson, G. N.: Anxiety and the alcoholic. *Q J Stud Alc, 32*: 976-981, 1971.
Horton, D.: The functions of alcohol in primitive societies. *Q J Stud Alc, 4*: 199-320, 1943.
Masserman, J. H., Yum, K. S., Nicholson, M. R., and Lee, S.: Neurosis and alcohol. *Am J Psychiatr, 101*: 389-395, 1944.
NIMH: *Alcohol and health.* Washington: U.S. Government Printing Office, 1971.
Petrie, A.: *Individuality in pain and suffering.* Chicago, University of Chicago, 1967.
Witkin, H. A.: Psychological differentiation and forms of pathology. *J Abnorm Psychol, 70*: 317-336, 1965.
Zarrow, M. X., Addus, H., and Denison, M.: Failure of the endocrine system to influence the alcoholic drive in rats. *Q J Stud Alc, 21*: 400-413, 1960.
Zax, M., and Cowen, E. L.: *Abnormal Psychology.* New York, Holt, Rinehart, and Winston, 1972.

CHAPTER 11 PSYCHOPATHS

IN RECENT YEARS three psychologists have turned their attention to psychopaths and delinquents and they have proposed three very different theories to account for antisocial behavior. As we examine each of these theories, it will become clear that each reduces to the same categorization of the psychopath or delinquent in the theoretical schema proposed in this book, namely that psychopaths or delinquents are S-type individuals.

DELINQUENTS AND REDUCING-AUGMENTING

Petrie (1967) discussed delinquents from the point of view of her personality dimension of reducing-augmenting (see Chapter 3). Petrie noted an atypical pattern of behavior in some of the subjects that she studied. When a large object was used for stimulation in the test of reducing-augmenting the individual reduced, but when a small object was used for stimulation the individual augmented. Petrie labeled this behavior "stimulus governed."

In a sample of seventy delinquent boys and girls and sixty-two non-delinquents, it was found that fourteen of the delinquents as compared to only three of the nondelinquents were stimulus governed. The stimulus governed delinquents had committed more prior offenses and were judged by their supervisors to be more immature, unpredictable, and changeable. They did not differ in intelligence, however.

Setting these stimulus governed delinquents aside, the remaining delinquents were found to be reducers much more often than were the nondelinquents, and they were more often extreme reducers. Thus, in the terminology of the present theory, delinquents would be categorized as S-types.

Petrie explored the implications of her finding that delinquents were, on the whole, reducers. It would be expected that delinquents would be more easily bored. They should be less well socialized since the rewards and punishments involved in socialization will not be as powerful for delinquents as they will be for nondelinquents. Their greater toleration for pain (which Petrie felt was manifest in their greater tolerance for tattooing and the painful process of removing unwanted tattoos) means that punishment will have less effect on them.

Petrie felt that delinquents learn less well than nondelinquents since there is a reduction in delinquents of afferent input. She felt that bedwetting is more common in delinquents (Michaels, 1955) since the cues providing information about bodily needs will be muted and often missed.

The greater tolerance for pain in delinquents will mean that they will be less able to empathize with the suffering of others. They may appear, therefore, to be sadistic and they may inflict pain on others without compunction. Furthermore, the delinquent may welcome pain himself since pain is, after all, a sensation and some sensation may be better than none. Thus, self-mutilating and masochistic behavior may be more common in delinquents.

As Petrie noted, these deductions have important implications for the rehabilitation of delinquents. Petrie noted that the most successful methods of rehabilitating delinquents have introduced them to physical challenges which maintain a high level of sensory stimulation.

EYSENCK'S THEORY OF PSYCHOPATHY

Eysenck's views on the structure of personality have been discussed in Chapter 4 above. Eysenck has extended his ideas to the criminal in the following manner. Eysenck suggested that socialized behavior (the opposite of antisocial or criminal behavior) depends upon classical conditioning which is applied during infancy and childhood to the individual by his parents, teachers, and peers. His behavior is then dependent upon the quantity and quality of the classical conditioning that he receives and the degree of conditionability that he possesses.

Many people refrain from criminal acts because of their conscience, their fear of the consequences of getting caught and punished for their antisocial behavior. Eysenck assumed that conscience is determined by classical conditioning (rather than by instrumental conditioning) and it would appear that the classical conditioning involved in the formation of a conscience involves the conditioning of fear, thus involving noxious unconditioned stimuli. (Eysenck noted that classical conditioning usually involved the autonomic nervous system whereas instrumental conditioning usually involved the central nervous system.) It might be noted in passing that avoidance learning has been thought by some investigators (e.g. Mowrer, 1960) to involve first a classical conditioning of the fear response and then instrumental conditioning based upon reduction of the classically conditioned fear. Thus, if classical conditioning is impaired in a person, then avoidance learning may also be impaired.

Eysenck saw the classical conditioning of fear responses as central to conscience since the punishments involved in criminal acts are often considerably delayed after the criminal acts, if the criminal is caught, which is not that often.

Eysenck (1963) has demonstrated psychopathic behavior in rats. He tried to teach rats to wait three seconds after a buzzer sounded before they approached and ate food. If they did not wait three seconds, they received an electric shock. Three reactions were found: the normal reaction was to wait three seconds and then proceed to the food, the neurotic reaction was to manifest extreme fear and never proceed to the food, and the psychopathic reaction was to brave the shock and proceed to the food immediately. Eysenck ran two strains of rats in the study. The nonemotional strain, on the whole, showed normal reactions, whereas the emotional strain showed neurotic and psychopathic reactions. If we can generalize from rats to humans, it appears that psychopaths may be highly emotional. But what distinguishes between the psychopath and the anxiety neurotic?

Eysenck suggested that psychopaths are extraverts (whereas anxiety neurotics are introverts). This has the implication (*see* Chapter 4) that psychopaths should classically condition less well than nonpsychopaths. Lykken (1957) has demonstrated this using the eyeblink response to a puff of air. Gibbens (1963) found that delinquent boys were less able to follow the rules for the Porteus Maze Test than were nondelinquents (and it has been found in other studies that extraverts contravene the rules more often than introverts).

A number of studies have shown that those who commit antisocial acts or delinquent acts are more extraverted than normal people. Fine (1963) reported that extraverted college students had had more traffic accidents than introverted college students. Eysenck (1961) found that unmarried mothers were more extraverted than married mothers. Syed (reported in Eysenck, 1964) studied female prisoners in England and found them to score high in both extraversion and neuroticism and data from Warburton (reported in Eysenck, 1964) on male prisoners in Chicago confirm this finding.

Eysenck noted that extraversion scales contain two kinds of items, those dealing with sociability and those dealing with impulsivity. The items dealing with impulsivity are those that differentiate psychopaths from nonpsychopaths best.

Studies on the drug treatment of antisocial persons support Eysenck's ideas. Cutts and Jasper (1949) found that behavior problems in a number of children were ameliorated by Benzedrine® and made worse by phenobarbital, a finding replicated by Lindsley and Henry (1942) and by Bradley and Bowen (1941). Eisenberg et al. (1963) carried out a well controlled study on delinquents and they found that delinquents adminstered amphetamine showed less delinquent behavior in the reformatory than delinquents given a placebo and those given nothing. In Eysenck's theory, stimulants uninhibit the central nervous system and, thus, move the individual toward introverted behavior.

Taking all these results together, it is clear that Eysenck has made a good case for the proposition that psychopaths are neurotic extraverts. As extraverts, therefore, they would be classified as S-types in the theoretical schema proposed in this book.

SCHACHTER'S THEORY OF PSYCHOPATHY

Schachter (1971) conducted a number of studies that indicated that emotions may be considered to be a function of the state of physiological arousal of the person and of cognitions appropriate to this state of arousel. In a typical study (Schachter and Singer, 1962), subjects injected with adrenalin (a sympathomimetic drug) became more euphoric in the presence of a happy person than did subjects injected with a placebo.

Turning to criminal acts, Schacter hypothesized that people fail to act upon their criminal impulses because they are restrained by fear. He deduced that, if he were to reduce the fear experienced by people through sympatholytic drugs, then criminal acts should become more common. Schachter tested this by injecting female subjects with either a sympatholytic drug (chlorpromazine) or a placebo under the guise of conducting a study on the effects of vitamins on perception. In the course of the study, the subjects were given the opportunity to grade examinations that they had taken for a course. The grading situation was arranged to encourage and to facilitate cheating by the subjects as they graded their own examinations. Schachter found that those subjects injected with chlorpromazine, and for whom the chlorpromazine had had a detectable physiological effect, cheated significantly more often than the other subjects.

Schachter felt that criminal acts could be divided into roughly two types: those committed because motivation or passion reached overwhelming intensity and those committed because the deterrents were feeble, deterrents such as the fear of the consequences. Those criminals who commit crimes apparently because their fear of the consequences of their acts is minimal are commonly known as psychopaths or sociopaths.

Lykken (1957) explored the relationship of anxiety to psychopathy. He demonstrated that psychopaths seemed relatively free from anxiety and he showed that psychopaths were virtually incapable of learning to avoid a painful stimulus (whereas normal subjects easily learnt this task). Lykken concluded that psychopaths were deficient in their ability to develop anxiety in response to warning cues.

Schachter developed these notions by examining the performance of psychopathic criminals and nonpsychopathic criminals on learning tasks involving positive reinforcement (making the correct response) and punishment (receiving electric shock for making particular errors). Subjects were given a maze to traverse with 20 choice-points. Each choice point contained four alternatives: one was correct, two were incorrect, and one was incorrect and, in addition, if the subject chose it he received an electric shock. The psychopaths and nonpsychopaths were tested under two conditions: after injections of adrenalin or after injections of a placebo (under the guise that the study was exploring the effects of vitamins on learning ability).

Examination of the number of correct responses made indicated that the psychopaths did not differ from the nonpsychopaths in the ease with which they learnt the correct responses. Furthermore, adrenalin had no effect on the ease of learning this task. However, examination of the particular errors made did disclose important differences.

In making errors, subjects were able to learn to avoid the error which would result in them receiving an electric shock. After injections of the placebo, the nonpsychopaths showed an ability to learn to avoid the shocked alternative, but the psychopaths did not show this ability. After injections of adrenalin, in contrast, the psychopaths showed an ability to learn to avoid the shocked alternative, but the nonpsychopaths did not show this ability.

Schachter concluded that something appeared to be amiss in the sympathetic systems of psychopaths. Adrenalin appears to remedy the defect. Schachter noted that the simplest explanation was that psychopaths are less sympathetically responsive. Their reduced sympathetic responsiveness should lead to emotional flatness and low anxiety, thus facilitating certain kinds of criminal acts.

However, data from his earlier studies indicated that the psychopaths tended to have a higher pulse rate than the nonpsychopaths and that adrenalin caused a larger increase in the pulse rate in the psychopaths than in the nonpsychopaths. This was found both in the study on cheating in undergraduates and in the study of avoidance learning in convicts. Valins (1963) conducted a study on college students to confirm this phenomenon. He measured psychopathy with a questionnaire devised by Lykken (1957) and subjected the students to pictures of grotesque facial injuries while measuring their heart rate and galvanic skin response. Students scoring high in psychopathy did not differ in their base measurements of heart rate and galvanic skin response, but the students scoring high in psychopathy did show a larger increase in the physiological measures to the visual stimuli than did the students scoring low in psychopathy.

In a final test of this phenomenon, Schachter monitored the heart rate of psychopathic and nonpsychopathic convicts using a telemetric EKG transmitter while he injected them with either a placebo or adrenalin (under the guise of a study of vitamins). During the pre-injection period, the psychopaths had somewhat higher heart rates than the nonpsychopaths. In response to the injection of the placebo, the psychopaths showed a greater increase in heart rate than did the nonpsychopaths. However, in response to the injection of adrenalin, the heart rate of the psychopaths jumped markedly as compared to the nonpsychopaths (from 88 beats per minute to 105 beats per minute as compared to a rise in the nonpsychopaths from 85 to 89 beats per minute).

Schachter concluded that psychopaths were more sympathetically responsive to a variety of stressful stimuli than are nonpsychopaths and that they are more sensitive to adrenalin than nonpsychopaths. It is clear that Schachter's original hypothesis that psychopaths have reduced sympathetic responsiveness was incorrect.

Schachter interpreted his finding in terms of labeling: how does the psychopath label his bodily sensations? Psychopaths appear to be more responsive to all stimuli, from the mildly provoking to the dangerously threatening. He responds sympathetically to events that are labeled as frightening by others and to events that are labeled as harmless by others. Schachter argued that indiscriminate reactivity is the equivalent of no reactivity. If every event arouses sympathetic activity, then the individual feels no differently during times of danger than during times of relative tranquility. Only intense states of sympathetic arousal (caused, for example, in Schachter's studies by injections of adrenalin) are noticeable and thus acquire emotional attributes for the psychopath. Thus, in short, psychopaths are characterized by marked sympathetic reactivity who, in the course of their development, learn not to apply emotional labels to their states of arousal. This sympathetic reactivity appears to be a result of an innate sensitivity to adrenalin.

It is clear, then, that according to Schachter's theory of psychopathy, psychopaths are S-type individuals.

It should be noted in passing that not all investigators agree with Schachter's thesis. Hare (1973) has reviewed a number of studies that have explored autonomic reactivity and learning in psychopaths. Measures of tonic autonomic reactivity of psychopaths in a resting state have indicated that, in general, psychopaths have a low level of resting tonic skin conductance and a relatively low level of nonspecific electrodermal activity. In addition, a few studies suggest that the mean tonic peak-trough difference in heart rate is lower in psychopaths.

Studies of autonomic responsivity to stimuli indicate that psychopaths are electrodermally hyporesponsive to intense stimuli, including electric shock and loud noise. There is some evidence also to suggest a reduced cardiac responsiveness to novel stimuli.

The learning deficit of psychopaths seems reasonably well-documented for two tasks: avoidance learning and classical conditioning of autonomic responses. A number of studies have demonstrated the poorer performance of psychopaths in avoiding electric shock (though they can learn to avoid responses leading to monetary loss). On classical conditioning tasks, the deficit in psychopaths is limited to classical conditioning tasks that involve electric shock as the unconditioned stimulus and the electrodermal response as the unconditioned response. The deficit of psychopaths is not found for cardiac or for vasomotor conditioning.

Thus, on the basis of his review of the literature and on the basis of his own studies, Hare concluded that psychopaths were marked by reduced sympathetic reactivity, thus disagreeing with Schachter.

PHYSIQUE AND DELINQUENCY

Studies of the body build of delinquents (as opposed to psychopaths) lend support to the notion that psychopaths are S-types. Sheldon (1949) categorized delinquents according to his constitutional theory of personality (see Chapter 9) and found that mesomorphy was more common among delinquents. Sutherland (1951) re-analyzed Sheldon's data and found a slight tendency for mesomorphic tendencies to increase and for ectomorphic tendencies to decrease with increasing criminality.

Glueck and Glueck (1956) compared delinquent and nondelinquent youths and found an excess of mesomorphs and a deficit of ectomorphs among the delinquents. The mesomorphic delinquents tended to have personality traits not commonly associated with mesomorphy, such as destructiveness, feelings of inadequacy, and emotional conflict. The Gluecks concluded that, when the mesomorph has traits disharmonious with his body type, then delinquency becomes a more likely outcome.

Studies by Epps and Parnell (1952), Gibbens (1963), and Cortes and Gatti (1970) have confirmed the association between delinquency and mesomorphy in both males and females and among delinquents in England and the United States of America.

In Chapter 9, evidence was presented that suggested that mesomorphs were S-types. Consequently, the data on the physique of delinquents suggests that delinquents are S-types.

Comment

It is evident that the three theories of psychopathy described in this chapter (those of Petrie, Eysenck, and Schachter) each lead us to categorize psychopaths as S-type individuals. The data from physique studies of psychopaths support this categorization.

It is of interest to speculate whether delinquents are N-subtypes or A-subtypes (see Chapter 8). Although Schachter used adrenalin to improve the performance of psychopaths at avoidance learning tasks and showed that they were sensitive to adrenalin, he has not yet studied the effects of noradrenalin. The data indicating that psychopaths are mesomorphs suggest that psychopaths are N-subtypes (see Chapter 9). Furthermore, Eysenck has noted that psychopaths are distinguished by the impulsivity items on scales of extraversion rather than by the sociability items. Sociability is more a characteristic of endomorphs than mesomorphs and, again, this datum suggests that psychopaths may be N-subtypes.

However, it may well prove that there are two major kinds of delinquents, N-subtypes and A-subtypes, and this distinction may have important consequences for etiology and rehabilitation.

REFERENCES

Bradley, C., and Bowen, M.: Amphetamine therapy of children's behavior disorders. *Am J Orthopsychiatry, 11*: 92-103, 1941.

Cortes, J., and Gatti, F.: Physique and propensity. *Psychol Today, 4*(5): 42-44, 82-84, 1970.

Cuts, K.K., and Jasper, H.H.: Effect of benzedrine sulfate on behavior-problem children with abnormal electroencephalograms. *Arch Neurol Psychiatr, 41*: 1138-1145, 1949.

Eisenberg, L., Lackman, R., Molling, P. A., Lockner, A., Mirelle, J. D., and Conners, C. K.: A psychopharmacologic experiment in a training school for delinquent boys. *Am J Orthopsychiatry, 33*: 431-447, 1963.

Epps, P., and Parnell, E. W.: Physiques and temperament of women delinquents compared with women undergraduates. *Br J Med Psychol, 25*: 249-255, 1952.

Eysenck, H. J.: Emotion as a determinant of integrative learning. *Beh Res Ther, 1*: 197-212, 1963.

Eysenck, H. J.: *Crime And Personality.* Boston, Houghton-Mifflin, 1964.

Eysenck, S. B. G.: Personality and pain assessemnt in childbirth of married and unmarried mothers. *J Ment Sci, 107*: 417-430, 1961.

Fine, B. J.: Introversion-extraversion and motor vehicle drive behavior. *Percept Mot Skills, 12*: 95-100, 1963.

Gibbens, T. C. N.: *Psychiatric Studies Of Borstal Lads.* London, Oxford University Press, 1963.

Glueck, S., and Glueck, E.: *Physique and Delinquency.* New York, Harper & Row, 1956.

Hare, R. D.: Autonomic activity and conditioning in psychopaths. In Maher, B. (Ed.): *Abnormal Psychology.* Baltimore, Penguin, 1973, pp. 224-251.

Lindsley, D. B., and Henry, C. E.: The effects of drugs on behavior and the electroencephalograms of children with behavior disorders. *Psychosom Med, 4*: 140-149, 1942.

Lykken, D.: A study of anxiety in the sociopathic personality. *J Abnorm Soc Psychol, 55*: 6-10, 1957.

Michaels, J. J.: *Disorders Of Character.* Springfeld, Charles C Thomas, 1955.

Mowrer, O. H.: *Learning Theory And The Symbolic Process.* New York, Wiley, 1960.

Petrie, A.: *Individuality In Pain And Suffering.* Chicago, University Of Chicago Press, 1967.

Schachter, S.: *Emotions, Obesity And Crime.* New York, Academic, 1971.

Schachter, S., and Singer, J. E.: Cognitive, social, and physiological determinants of emotional state. *Psychol Rev, 69*: 379-399, 1962.

Sheldon, W. H.: *Varieties Of Delinquent Youth.* New York: Harper & Row, 1949.

Sutherland, E. H.: Critique of Sheldon's "Varieties of delinquent youth." *Am Soc Rev, 16*: 10-13, 1951.

Valins, S.: Psychopathy and physiological reactivity under stress. Master's thesis, Columbia University, 1963.

CHAPTER 12 PSYCHOSIS

PETRIE'S THEORY OF SCHIZOPHRENIA

PETRIE'S WORK on the personality dimension of reducing-augmenting was discussed in Chapter 3. As a result of her numerous studies, Petrie concluded that schizophrenics were reducers. Not only this, but the reducing tendencies were extremely persistent. However, a number of the schizophrenics showed extreme swings from test to test session between extreme reducing and extreme augmenting.

Petrie noted that her finding was consistent with reports that schizophrenics mutilate themselves frequently, often without reacting to the pain that must be involved (Lester, 1972). Petrie also noted that dysmenorrhea was rarely reported by schizophrenics, although it was common in the staff of psychiatric hospitals.

Petrie speculated that the extreme reducing of the schizophrenic might be a learned response. She suggested that schizophrenics were born as augmenters, and perhaps as extreme augmenters. This had the result that they were confronted with more sensory bombardment than they could tolerate. They learnt to reduce as a defense, but they were unable to learn to moderately reduce. Rather, they learnt to go into what Petrie called "spasms" of reducing. Even so, there are phases during their illness when they return to their natural augmenting state temporarily. Petrie noted that schizophrenics are often reported to have originally been persons of "exquisite sensibility" and often showed pathological hyperesthesia. This ties in with the reports by Bergman and Escalona (1949) and Korner (1971) of children with unusual sensitivities who generally become psychotic in later life.

In the extreme reducing state of the schizophrenic, the world may also be unbearable, not because of what is perceived, but because of what is not perceived. The person has a new problem, a kind of sensory deprivation. Psychotic experiences can be seen as attempts to create a world in which the schizophrenic can live. Hallucinations serve to increase sensory input during periods of sensory lack, for example. Petrie noted that, if her speculations were correct, then it would be necessary to protect schizophrenics from overbombardment from stimuli as they return to a normal state.

McREYNOLDS' THEORY OF SCHIZOPHRENIA

The studies of Petrie that suggest that schizophrenics were born as extreme augmenters and, thus, that they are P-types is nicely complemented by a theory of schizophrenia proposed by McReynolds (1960) that gives a detailed explanation of the development of a schizophrenic state.

McReynolds' model of normal functioning focusses upon how we perceive the world. The units of analysis are *percepts,* data that pass through an individual's awareness and remain with him. Mental life is conceived of as (a) obtaining and receiving percepts and (b) assimilating or integrating these percepts.

There are two sources of percepts, chance and percepts actively sought by the individual. In order to account for the later source of percepts, McReynolds postulated the existence of an innate tendency to seek percepts, a need which has often been proposed to account for curiosity and exploratory behavior (Lester, 1969).

The percepts received by the individual are assimilated, that is, they enter harmoniously and congruently into systematic conjunction with percept previously experienced. Assimilation entails categorization of percepts and the fitting of them into conceptual schemata, enduring plans for the ordering of percepts. Some percepts may fit into existing schemata easily. Others may require restructuring of existing schemata, while still others may require the construction of new schemata. Incongruency refers to those characteristics of percepts that make assimilation difficult.

If percepts remain unassimilated, then anxiety is generated in the individual. The greater the number of unassimilated percepts, the higher the level of anxiety. Four factors make assimilation of percepts difficult and thus result in anxiety: (1) a too high a rate of influx of percepts, (2) extremely novel percepts which require considerable restructuring of schemata and thus retard assimilation, (3) additional percepts necessary for assimilation are not presently available, and (4) incongruencies in the percepts being received.

McReynolds proposed that schizophrenia results from a condition of overwhelming anxiety. This is caused by a high level of unassimilated percepts. Why might an individual obtain a high level of unassimilated percepts that would facilitate his schizophrenic breakdown? Two possibilities exist. One is that the parents of schizophrenics are more prone to utter double-bind communications, communications with more than one level in which the meaning of the different levels is in conflict. For example, a mother tells her child "But of course mommy loves you" while the tone of her voice belies this fact. Double-bind communications will be hard to assimilate (Lester, 1968). However, empirical support for the double-bind theory of schizophrenia is not good at the present time (Schuham, 1967).

A second possibility is that, as Petrie suggested, schizophrenics as children were bombarded with more percepts than they could handle. Thus, the percepts remained unassimilated and so generated anxiety. Augmenters may be more likely to be overbombarded and so develop unassimilated percepts, thus becoming more anxious.

This theory can explain many of the schizophrenic symptoms. A person who has a large number of unassimilated percept will try to keep the quantity of unassimilated percepts as low as possible. Thus he may show withdrawal, avoidance, and apathy. He will show avoidance responses particularly with regard to those percepts related to those areas in which he has a good deal of incongruency. Byrne *et al* (reported in McReynolds, 1960) showed that psychiatric patients with incongruency in particular areas such as hostility were less likely to perceive hostility and to perceive it accurately in cartoons. Furthermore, Bryan and McReynolds (1956) also showed that psychiatric patients with higher levels of unassimilated percepts in a laboratory task were less likely to choose novel stimuli.

McReynolds noted that a low rate of perceptualization (that is, receiving and assimilating percepts) impairs intellectual performance (as in studies of sensory deprivation [Bexton *et al.*, 1954]). Thus, schizophrenics who show withdrawal would be expected to have impaired intellectual activity and, in particular, impaired organized and directed thinking.

Similarly, the reduced perceptualization rate in schizophrenics should make hallucinations more likely, since hallucinations seem to occur when the brain is deprived of adequate external stimulation. Of course, in hallucinations the individual fails to discriminate whether the stimulus is from within himself or whether it is "out there." This aspect of the phenomenon is more difficult to incorporate into McReynolds' theory.

Efforts to assimilate the unassimilated percepts underlie other symptoms. Because some of his percepts are assimilated, the schizophrenic will be reluctant to restructure his schemata (or beliefs). He may thus appear to be rigid. Delusions, beliefs that observers feel to be erroneous, can be seen as desperate attempts to provide schemata which can serve to assimilate some of the unassimilated percepts. Furthermore, assimilation can be facilitated if the schizophrenic is loose in his application of categorizations, which leads to behaviors known as overinclusion (Cameron, 1947).

It can be seen that McReynolds' theory of schizophrenia can provide a rational explanation for the development of schizophrenia, especially if Petrie's ideas on schizophrenics as augmenters (and thus as P-types) are adopted as part of the rationale.

EMPIRICAL STUDIES OF SCHIZOPHRENICS

Empirical studies of schizophrenics tend to be somewhat inconsistent, and this appears to be due to the heterogeneity of schizophrenics. A difference that is relevant to the present thesis is that between paranoid schizophrenics and nonparanoid schizophrenics. For example, Witkin (1965), in reviewing psychopathological correlates of his dimension of field dependence/field independence (or more broadly, global versus articulated styles of cognitive functioning) noted that the evidence indicated that catatonic schizophrenics and hallucinating schizophrenics were field dependent (and thus functioning as S-types) while paranoid schizophrenics and ambulatory schizophrenics with a well-developed defensive structure were field independent. (There is some data, though not as consistent, to indicate that process schizophrenics are field dependent while reactive schizophrenics are field independent.) This finding is consistent with Petrie's report that schizophrenics act as if they were reducers.

Silverman (1967) reviewed research relative to two cognitive dimensions in schizophrenics, sensitivity to sensory input and scanning of the stimulus situation, and again noted the difference between paranoid and nonparanoid schizophrenics. Studies of figural after-effects, sensory thresholds, reaction times to stimuli, and pain tolerance tests indicate that nonparanoid schizophrencis (and chronic, process schizophrenics) show reducing tendencies. Paranoid schizophrenics, on the other hand, do not show reducing tendencies.

Rubin (1962) has suggested that an adrenergic-cholinergic unbalance is an important aspect of functional psychosis and Lang and Buss (1965) have reviewed investigations of somatic arousal in schizophrenics. In general, studies of the habitual level of somatic arousal are consistent. Studies of the cardiovascular and neuromuscular systems point to a heightened level of arousal. Studies of skin resistance are inconsistent (and, in particular, do not support the conclusion of Wenger *et al.* [1956] that the autonomic activity of schizophrenics is dominated by the sympathetic system). However, Solomon *et al.* (1939) noted that sweat gland activity, though sympathetically activated, is a cholinergic mechanism.

Studies of reactivity to stimulation are also consistent (Lang and Buss, 1965). Psychomotor, vestibular, sweat gland, and cortical electroencephalogram responses are reduced relative to normal subjects in schizophrenics. This is more marked in chronic and process schizophrenics than in acute and reactive schizophrenics, and the findings do not seem valid for relatively intact paranoid schizophrenics and perhaps not for early schizophrenics.

These findings lend considerable support to Petrie's speculations and the present theory. Schizophrenics should behave like S-types, that is, have a sympathetic predominance in their autonomic nervous system and act like reducers. The data confirm this. In addition, schizophrenics in the pre-morbid state should be augmenters and P-types and the data from early schizophrenics (Malmo and Shagass, 1949) appears to support this notion.

One way in which the empirical data do require a modification of the theory is that paranoid schizophrenics must be removed from the theory. This later conclusion fits in well with the physique studies of Sheldon (1942) who reported that nonparanoid schizophrenics were ectomorphic (and thus P-types) while paranoid schizophrenics were mesomorphic (and thus S-types, subtype N).

These conclusions agree in part with Russian research on schizophrenia (Lynn, 1963). Russian investigators have noted that there is a depression of sympathetic system activity in simple and catatonic schizophrenics, both in its level and in its reactivity to stimulation. Stimulants such as caffeine and atropine improve sympathetic tone and reactivity. In contrast, acute, agitated, and paranoid schizophrenics have a high level of sympathetic arousal and reactivity.

Russian reports indicate that classical conditioning is poor in simple and catatonic schizophrenics, more so than in paranoid schizophrenics. Again, atropine in small doses improves the schizophrenics' performance on conditioning tasks.

The research by Rubin (1962), mentioned briefly above, indicates that the picture may be quite complex. Rubin noted that adrenergic and cholinergic functioning seems to be abnormal in functional psychotics. For example, Rubin noted that Iproniazid® (an adrenergic drug) helps some depressive psychotics, whereas reserpine and chlorpromazine (which are adrenergic depressants) improve the performance of some schizophrenics. The cholinergic system is implicated by the finding that atropine (a cholinergic depressant) improves the performance of some psychotics in manic states.

Rubin attempted to assess adrenergic functioning and cholinergic functioning by noting the pupil response to the offset of light and the onset of light respectively. Using these measures he classified subjects as showing excessive, normal, and deficient in each of the systems, adrenergic and cholinergic. Normal persons would obtain normal scores for both adrenergic and cholinergic functioning. In tests of 71 functional psychotics, Rubin found not one single psychotic that received normal scores for both adrenergic and cholinergic functioning.

Rubin's technique allows us to classify eight kinds of disordered adrenergic-cholinergic functioning. Rubin did not speculate as to which types of psychotics fall into each of the eight possible kinds of imbalance, but subsequent research may provide some answers here.

BIOCHEMICAL THEORIES OF SCHIZOPHRENIA

Cholinergic Theories

Biochemical theories of schizophrenia have had notoriously short lives in the past, and it is not the intent here to present some biochemical theories as if they were valid. The intent is to point out that biochemical theories, as well as psychological theories, have occasionally sought to implicate the autonomic nervous system.

Before describing some of these, it is necessary to outline the production of acetylcholine in the cholinergic system of the autonomic nervous system.

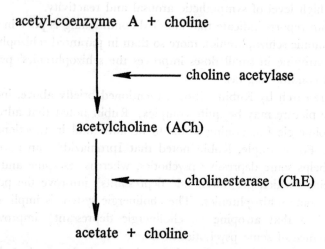

acetyl-coenzyme A + choline

choline acetylase

acetylcholine (ACh)

cholinesterase (ChE)

acetate + choline

For the transmission of nerve impulses in the cholinergic system, small amounts of acetylcholine (ACh) are necesary, but ACh must not accumulate. The enzyme cholinesterase (ChE) hydrolyzes ACh and inactivates it rapidly after its release.

Russell (1958) noted that when patients in chronic catatonic stupor are given ChE, they improve so much that eventually they can take care of their own needs (Feldberg and Sherwood, 1955). Experimental catatonia can be produced by the presence of various anticholinesterase drugs or by the presence of large quantities of ACh in the ventricles of the brain. Hoffer (1957) too has suggested that one basic condition necessary for the appearance of schizophrenia was an increase in the concentration of ACh in the brain.

Animal work supports these findings. Russell (1958) reported that drugs which reduce the concentration of ChE also lead to impairment in serial problem solving ability, adjustment to environmental stresses, and extinction, but had no effect on locomotion, simple learning, instrumental conditioning, and visual discrimination. (This phenomenon will be discussed again in Chapter 18 when the work of Broverman et al. [1968] on sex differences in perceptual-motor functioning will be discussed.)

On the other hand, Pfeiffer *et al.* (1957) gave cholinergic agents in large quantities to schizophrenics and obtained amelioration of their symptoms. He suggested that schizophrenia was due to a lack of ACh in the brain. Pfeiffer and Jenney (1957) suggested that an increase in ACh may have an antischizophrenic effect. In line with this, Jacobsen (1955) noted that benactyzine, which blocks ACh, has no effect on schizophrenics.

The evidence therefore is not consistent. It may be, of course, that the different groups of investigators are studying different kinds of schizophrenics (chronic versus acute, etc.) However, at the present time, the discrepancies remain unresolved.

Adrenergic Theories

Adrenergic theories of schizophrenia have perhaps fared less well than cholinergic theories (Kety, 1959). Osmond (1955) and Hoffer (1957) tried to relate the pathogenesis of schizophrenia to the faulty metabolism of adrenalin. The symptoms of the disease were attributed to the action of abnormal hallucinogenic derivatives of adrenalin, called adrenolutin and adrenochrome. This faulty metabolism was thought to be triggered by both genetic and environmental factors.

There was some evidence that some of the oxidation products of adrenalin were psychomimetic (Osmond, 1955) but, not only did other investigators fail to confirm this (eg. Rinkel and Solomon, 1957), but also the original proponents were often unable to confirm their earlier results (Kety, 1959).

Other investigators claimed to find that adrenalin was oxidized faster by schizophrenics (Leach and Heath, 1956) and Hoffer and Kenyon (1957) reported that the oxidized products were adrenolutin. Kety has noted, however, that the major metabolites of adrenalin have been identified in recent years and that adrenolutin and adrenochrome do not appear to be included in these metabolites. Furthermore, other investigators have failed to find adrenolutin and adrenochrome in the blood of normal subjects, acute schizophrenics or chronic schizophrenics (Szara *et al.,* 1958). In addition, the administration of adrenalin to schizophrenics, which should exacerbate their symptoms, appears to have no effect (Heath *et al.*, 1958).

Kety noted, politely, that none of this negative evidence invalidates the adrenalin theories of schizophrenia. It does, however, weaken the evidence adduced to support the theories.

Comment

It is perhaps worth noting that, of the two kinds of theories, those based on cholinergic mechanisms seem to fare better than those based on adrenergic mechanisms. This fits in with the thesis of the present book that schizophrenics are basically P-type individuals who function as if they are S-type individuals. This means that the physiological characteristics of (nonparanoid) schizophrenics should manifest a degree of parasympathetic dominance, while the psychological behavior should resemble that of individuals with sympathetic dominance.

Snyder (1972) has proposed a recent biochemical theory for paranoid schizophrenia that is consistent with the above opinions and research. Snyder noted the similarity between the symptoms of paranoid schizophrenia and the symptoms of amphetamine-induced psychotic behavior. Amphetamine is a sympathomimetic drug, that is, it stimulates the sympathetic system and Snyder has tentatively suggested that excessive use of amphetamine produces symptoms of paranoid schizophrenia by affecting the noradrenalin tracts of the brain. Snyder has speculated that excessive activity of the dopamine neural pathways leads to general symptoms of schizophrenia, while excessive activity of the noradrenalin pathways leads to symptoms such as hyperactivity, sleeplessness, and loss of appetite. This alerting effect may lead the patient to seek an intellectual framework for his feelings and behavior which may lead him to elaborate delusional schemata. Snyder has predicted that, if a drug that affects only the dopamine pathways is discovered, then this drug would produce symptoms of nonparanoid schizophrenia.

MANIC-DEPRESSIVE PSYCHOSIS

Beck (1967) has reviewed a number of studies purporting to show differences between those with psychotic depressions and those with neurotic depressions. In general, Beck noted that depressed psychotics are older than depressed neurotics and that, when this difference in age is controlled, the differences reported by these studies are eliminated.

For example, those with manic-depressive psychosis are found to have reduced salivation (a characteristic of sympathetic dominance). However, Beck noted that the studies on this had failed to control for age, oral disease, smoking habits, and so on. Hemphill *et al.* (1952) found depressed psychiatric patients to have a higher threshold for pain (which would make them reducers and thus S-types), but again Beck noted that the depressed patients were older than the nondepressed patients.

A number of studies have reported that those with manic-depressive psychosis are more endomorphic than those with other diagnoses. Rees (1944) reported that the increased endomorphy of the manic-depressives over schizophrenics was explained partially by age differences, but not completely. However, Beck thought that the longer hospitalization of the schizophrenics might have caused greater physical deterioration in them as compared to the manic-depressives.

Funkenstein (1954) has reported that manic-depressives respond with an adrenalin response to stress (see Chapter 8) and Shagass *et al.* (1956) reported that the sedation threshold was lower in those diagnosed as depressed psychotics. These findings have not yet been replicated by independent investigators (and again age was not controlled for in the studies). In addition, with respect to Funkenstein's report, Curtis *et al.* (1960) reported that adrenalin excretion was lower in depressed psychiatric patients whereas the excretion of noradrenalin was higher.

Although Beck felt that these differences were of doubtful validity, two things may be noted. First, even if age is a confounding variable, the thesis that manic-depressives are S-types may not be negated. For example, if people become more endomorphic with increasing age and if manic-depressive disease becomes more common with increasing age, then perhaps the two variables are causally related.

Secondly, the reports of the characteristics of manic-depressives all suggest the placement of manic-depressives as S-types. Endomorphy, a higher threshold for pain, and dryness of the mouth are all characteristics of S-type individuals, as is a lower sedation threshold. Furthermore, endomorphy and a reaction of anger-in to stress are both characteristic of S-type individuals, subtype A. Thus, the findings, though not reliable, are consistent with one another.

It is also interesting to note that one biochemical theory of depression is consistent with the present thesis. The catecholamine theory (Schildkraut, 1965) has as a central idea the notion that the supply of active noradrenalin is centrally depleted in depression. (This might account for the excess excretion of noradrenalin in depressives noted by Curtis *et al.* [1960].) This lends partial support to the categorization of depressed psychotics as subtype A, if we can assume that they are S-types.

CONCLUSIONS

A review of available data and current theories has led to the categorization of manic-depressives as S-type individuals, subtype A and to the categorization of schizophrenics as P-types who are behaving like extreme S-types as part of a defense process. Paranoid individuals appear to be S-types, subtype N.

The thesis with respect to schizophrenics points to a possibility that is interesting but which poses logical problems. Nonparanoid schizophrenics behave as if they were S-types, but they have been categorized as individuals who were born as P-types. In order to adapt to the stresses that they were subject to, they acted defensively as S-types. This kind of argument could easily lead to *post hoc* explanations. For example, why were manic-depressives not categorized as individuals who were born as P-types who later switched and began to act like S-type individuals? The validity of the hypothesis about schizophrenics can be tested only by longitudinal studies in which it is possible to administer the crucial tests both prior to and after the schizophrenic breakdown.

REFERENCES

Beck, A. T.: *Depression.* New York, Hoeber, 1967.

Bergman, P., and Escalona, S.: Unusual sensitivities in very young children. *Psychoan Studies Child, 3/4*: 333-352, 1949.

Bexton, W., Heron, W., and Scott, T.: Effects of decreased variation in the sensory environment. *Canad J Psychol, 8*: 70-76, 1954.

Broverman, D., Klaiber, E., Kobayashi, Y., and Vogel, W.: Roles of activation and inhibition in sex differences in cognitive abilities. *Psychol Rev, 75*: 23-50, 1968.

Bryan, J., and McReynolds, P.: The tendency to obtain new percepts as a function of the level of unassimilated percepts. *Percept Mot Skills, 6*: 183-186, 1956.

Cameron, N.: *The Psychology Of Behavior Disorders.* Boston, Houghton-Mifflin, 1947.

Curtis, G. C., Cleghorn, R. A., and Sourkes, T. L.: The relationship between affect and the excretion of adrenaline, noradrenaline, and 17-hydroxycortico-steroids. *J Psychosom Res, 4*: 176-184, 1960.

Feldberg, W., and Sherwood, S.: Recent experiments with injections of drugs into the ventricular system of the brain. *Proc Roy Soc Med., 48*: 853-864, 1955.

Funkenstein, D. H.: The physiology of fear and anger. *Sci Am, 192(5)*: 74-80, 1955.

Heath, R. G., Leach, B. E., Byers, L. W., Martens, S., and Feigley C. A.: Pharmacological and biological psychotherapy. *Am J Psychiatr, 114*: 683-689, 1958.

Hemphill, R. E., Hall, K. R., and Crookes, T. G. : A preliminary report on fatigue and pain tolerance in depressive and psychoneurotic patients. *J Ment Sci, 98*: 433-440, 1952.

Hoffer, A.: Epinephrine derivatives as potential schizophrenic factors. *J Clin Exp Psychopath, 18*: 27-60, 1957.

Hoffer, A., and Kenyon, M.: Conversion of adrenaline to adrenolutin in human blood serum. *Arch Neurol Psychiatr, 77*: 437-438, 1957.

Jacobsen, E.: A new drug effective on the central nervous system. *Danish Med Bull, 2*: 159-160, 1955.

Kety, S. S.: Biochemical theories of schizophrenia. *Science, 129*: 1528-1532, 1959.

Korner, A. F.: Individual differences at birth. *Am J Orthopsychiatr, 41*: 608-619, 1971.

Lang, P. J., and Buss, A. H.: Psychological deficit in schizophrenia. *J Abnorm Psychol, 70*: 77-106, 1965.

Leach, B. E., and Heath, R. G.: The *in vitro* oxidation of epinephrine in plasma. *Arch Neurol Psychiatr, 76*: 444-450, 1956.

Lester, D.: The double-bind hypothesis and the failure to assimilate. *Psychol Rep, 23*: 520, 1968.

Lester, D.: *Explorations in exploration.* Princeton: Van Nostrand, 1969.

Lester, D.: Self-mutilating behavior. *Psychol Bull, 78*: 119-128, 1972.

Lynn, R.: Russian theory and research on schizophrenia. *Psychol Bull, 60*: 486-498, 1963.

Malmo, R. B., and Shagass, C.: Physiological studies of reaction to stress in anxiety states and early schizophrenia. *Psychosom Med, 11*: 9-24, 1949.

McReynolds, P.: Anixety, perception and schizophrenia. In Jackson, D. (Ed.): *The Etiology Of Schizophrenia.* New York, Basic, 1960, pp. 248-292.

Osmond, H.: Inspiration and method in schizophrenia research. *Dis Nerv Sys, 16*: 101-110, 1955.

Petrie, A.: *Individuality In Pain And Suffering.* Chicago, University of Chicago Press, 1967.

Pfeiffer, C., and Jenney, E.: The inhibition of the conditioned response and the counteraction of schizophrenia by muscarinic stimulation of the brain. *Ann N Y Acad Sci, 66*: 753-764, 1957.

Pfeiffer, C., Jenney, E., Gallagher, W., Smith, R., Bevan, W., Killam, K., Killam, E., and Blackmore, W.: Stimulant effect of 2-dimethylaminoethanol. *Science, 126*: 610-611, 1957.

Rees, L.: Physical constiution, neurosis and psychosis. *Proc Roy Soc Med, 37*: 635-638, 1944.

Rinkel, M., and Solomon, H. C.: Chemical theories of psychosis. *J Clin Exp Psychopathol, 18*: 323-334, 1957.

Rubin, L.: Patterns of adrenergic-cholinergic imbalance in the functional psychoses. *Psychol Rev, 69*: 501-519, 1962.

Russell, R. W.: Drugs as tools in behavioral research. In Uhr, L. and Miller, J. G. (Eds.): *Drugs And Behavior.* New York, Wiley, 1960. pp. 19-40.

Schildkraut, J.: The catecholamine hypothesis of affective disorders. *Am J Psychiatr, 122*: 509-522, 1965.

Schuham, A. I.: The double-bind hypothesis a decade later. *Psychol Bull, 68*: 409-416, 1967.

Shagass, C., Naiman, J., and Mihalik, J.: An objective test which differentiates between neurotic and psychotic depression. *Arch Neurol Psychiatr, 75*: 461-471, 1956.

Sheldon, W. H.: *The Varieties Of Temperament.* New York, Harper, 1942.

Silverman, J.: Variations in cognitive control and psychophysiological defense in the schizophrenias. *Psychosom Med, 29*: 225-251, 1967.

Snyder, S.: The true speed trip. *Psychol Today, 5*(8): 42-46, 74-75, 1972.

Solomon, A. P., Darrow, C. W., and Blaurock, M.: Blood pressure and palmar sweat (galvanic) responses of psychotic patients before and after insulin and metrazol therapy. *Psychosom Med, 1*: 118-137, 1939.

Szara, S., Axelrod, J., and Perlin, S.: Is adrenochrome present in the blood? *Amer J Psychiatr, 115*: 162-163, 1958.

Wenger, M. A., Jones, N. F., and Jones, M .H.: *Psychological Psychology.* New York, Holt, 1956.

Witkin, H. A.: Psychological differentiation and forms of pathology. *J Abnorm Psychol, 70*: 317-336, 1965.

CHAPTER 13 NEUROSIS

T HE NEUROSES are a disparate group of disorders and they appear to differ considerably with respect to their involvement with the autonomic nervous system. The personality theory developed by Eysenck (1957) (see Chapter 4) provides a good classificatory system for the neuroses that seems relevant to the autonomic system as well. Eysenck saw hysteria as one kind of neurosis and phobias, anxiety neurosis, and obsessional-compulsive neurosis as a very different kind. The latter three neurotic disorders have been called dysthymia by Eysenck.

Eysenck has proposed that hysterics are neurotic extraverts while dysthymics are neurotic introverts. Templer and Lester (1974) have reviewed the research relevant to this proposition and, on the whole, it supports Eysenck's theory. Certainly dysthmics do appear to obtain high scores on tests of neuroticism and low scores on tests of extraversion. Hysterics, however, though obtaining high scores on tests of neuroticism, appear to obtain average scores on tests of extraversion. Thus, although hysterics are certainly more extraverted than dysthymics, they are not extremely extraverted. Ingham and Robinson (1964) noted that patients with hysterical personalities are extremely extraverted and they suggested that those with hysterical personalities fitted Eysenck's theory better than hysterics. However, as Templer and Lester have noted, the majority of hysterics do not have hysterical personalities. The two disorders do not appear to be similar.

If Eysenck's theory is correct then hysterics should condition less easily, have better and longer figural after-effects, and perform worse at clerical and sorting tasks. The current research appears to support these predictions well (Templer and Lester, 1974). For example, hysterics condition less well in a verbal conditioning task (Gelfand and Winder, 1961) and show better and longer figural after-effects (Eysenck, 1955).

In daily behavior, hysterics do appear to resemble extraverts. They draw less compactly, have a greater preference for modern paintings, and appreciate jokes more (Templer and Lester, 1974). Finally, it is interesting to note that many hysterical symptoms are related to reducing behavior: analgesia, anesthesia, blindness, deafness, and so forth.

An independent source of evidence connecting hysteria to extraversion comes from studies of antisocial behavior and hysteria. Templer and Lester (1974) have noted that the two behaviors appear to be associated and they suggested that they have a common etiology. However, the appearance of the disorders is sex-linked, with females showing hysterical disorders more while males show antisocial disorders (or psychopathy or delinquency) more.

For example, the male relatives of female hysterics tend to have a high incidence of antisocial behavior and alcoholism whereas the female relatives of female hysterics have a high incidence of hysteria (Woerner and Guze, 1968). Guze *et al.* (1967) have reported a high incidence of hysteria in the female relatives of male criminals.

Furthermore, females with behavior problems frequently are diagnosed as hysterics when seen as adults and female hysterics commonly have a personal history of delinquency and antisocial behavior.

It may be concluded that the evidence that hysterics are extraverts (and thus S-types) whereas dysthymics are introverts (and thus P-types) is reasonably good.

In fairness, it should be noted that studies of autonomic functioning do not support this conclusion. Wenger (1966) has reported that anxiety neurotics have sympathetic predominance, a conclusion reached by Merwe (1948) after a study of peripheral vasomotor reactions.*

The differences between the studies of extraversion and those of autonomic balance cannot be reconciled as yet. It might be noted that Perley and Guze (1962) have set criteria for a diagnosis of hysteria that are rarely applied. Many investigators are studying individuals with conversion symptoms rather than individuals with the clinical syndrome of hysteria. Secondly, the grouping together of all other neurotics may not be a sound methodological procedure and

---

*In this connection, it is interesting to note that Jacobsen (1955) has implicated anxiety and phobic neuroses (dysthymics) with the cholinergic system by showing that benactyzine, which blocks ACh, functions as an antiphobic drug, reducing abnormal fears and emotional reactivity to stress.

the control groups in studies by different investigators may differ considerably.

Be that as it may, the data on the relationship between neuroses and the balance in the autonomic nervous system is presently far from clear.

REFERENCES

Eysenck, H. J.: Cortical inhibition, figural after-effects, and theory of personality. *J Abnorm Soc Psychol, 51*: 94-106, 1955.

Eysenck, H. J.: *The dynamics of anxiety and hysteria.* New York, Praeger, 1957.

Gelfand, D. M., and Winder, C. L.: Operant conditioning of verbal behavior of dysthymics and hysterics. *J Abnorm Soc Psychol, 62*: 688-689, 1961.

Guze, S. B., Wolfgram, E. D., McKinney, I. K., and Cantwell, D. P.: Psychiatric illness in the families of convicted criminals. *Dis Nerv Sys, 28*: 651-659, 1967.

Ingham, J. G., and Robinson, J. O.: Personality in the diagnosis of hysteria. *Br J Psychol, 55*: 276-284, 1964.

Jacobsen, E.: A new drug effective on the central nervous system. *Danish Med Bull, 2*: 159-160, 1955.

Merwe, A.: The diagnostic value of peripheral vasomotor reactions in the psychoneuroses. *Psychosom Med, 10*: 347-354.

Perley, M. J., and Guze, S. B.: Hysteria. *New Eng J Med, 266*: 421-426, 1962.

Templer, D. I., and Lester, D.: Conversion disorders. In preparation, 1974.

Wenger, M. A.: Studies of autonomic balance. *Psychophysiol, 2*: 173-186, 1966.

Woerner, P. I., and Guze, S. B.: A family and marital study of hysteria. *Br J Psychiatr, 114*: 161-168, 1968.

CHAPTER 14
VOODOO DEATH AND SUDDEN DEATH*

IT HAS FREQUENTLY BEEN OBSERVED that members of primitive societies have died under the influence of a "voodoo" or a "hex." For example, Spencer and Gillin (1899) reported that members of the tribes in Central Australia often attributed deaths to the use of a poison bone. All that was necessary was for an enemy to point the bone at you and intone a course for a rapid death to overtake you.

The notion of voodoo has been questioned. Barber (1961) felt that many cases of voodoo death might have involved poisoning of the victim or organic disease. Many cases of voodoo death are based on hearsay, rather than direct observation, and so the reports are open to distortion. In cases of voodoo death that have been observed, it is noticed that often the victims refuse food and water, and this may hasten (if not directly cause) death. However, if an intonation or curse can lead someone to refuse nourishment so that he dies, then this is indeed a valid case of death by suggestion.

Many writers on voodoo death commonly assume that death by suggestion is a phenomenon found only in primitive societies. This is not so. The phenomenon can be found in more developed societies and in modern times. Richter (1957) noted a parallel phenomenon reportedly found among the black population in the southern states of this country.

THEORIES OF VOODOO DEATH

Cannon (1942) reported work that he had carried out in men and animals on sudden death. Cannon observed that, when cats were decorticated, they behaved as if they were in a state of rage. They had a very low threshold for the arousal of rage behavior, and the rage, when elicited, was not directed toward the frustrating agent but

---

*This chapter is based on Lester (1972).

[84]

at random. This behavior was called "sham rage" to indicate its similarities to true rage and to emphasize its differences.

Cannon noted that cats occasionally died after showing intense sham rage and his studies indicated that death was the result of overstimulation of the sympathetic system. Cannon felt that voodoo death in man bore a close resemblance to sudden death in decorticate cats, and he suggested that a similar physiological mechanism might be operating in both cases. Individuals dying under the influence of a hex may die as a result of overstimulation of the sympathetic system. Prolonged hyperactivity of the sympathetic system reinforced by the effects of adrenalin released from the adrenal medulla, accompanied by loss of blood plasma into the interstitial space of the gastrointestinal tract results in a state of hypovolemic shock. Cannon was able to find instances of death in man due to hypovolemic shock following minor nonlethal injuries.

Richter (1957) came to the study of voodoo death via his work on rats. He found that, after trimming the fur and whiskers of rats with clippers, some died within a few hours. He investigated the physiological concomitants of sudden death in wild rats under stress, who succumb in this manner much more often than domesticated rats, and concluded that, contrary to Cannon's belief, death appeared to result from hyperactivity of the parasympathetic system. The heart rate of the animals appeared to decrease after the stress was applied and, on autopsy, the heart was found to be filled with blood.

If domesticated rats were injected with cholinergic drugs which, in general, have a parasympathomimetic effect, then they too showed the phenomenon of sudden death under stress. Similarly, atropine (a parasympatholytic drug) reduces the incidence of sudden death in wild rats under stress.

Richter speculated that the stressful situation in which he placed his rats (whiskers trimmed, restrained in a jar filled with water) allowed the rats no opportunity for escape. They could not flee or fight (reactions mediated by the sympathetic system). He suggested that the situation was one of hopelessness, and the animals behaved as if they had literally given up. Richter concluded, therefore, that, by analogy, victims of voodo death die a parasympathetic death of hopelessness.*

---

*A more adequate theory of voodoo death has been presented by Lester (1972).

SUDDEN DEATH

The phenomen of sudden death in humans has been noted for many years now. In a recent review of cases of sudden death, Dynes (1969) noted that there were two types, both occurring without significant anatomical findings at autopsy. One type follows prolonged excitement and violence whereas the other type occurs instantaneously and without warning. The following is a case reported by Dynes.

One patient, 26 years of age had been violent and difficult to control intermittently over a four-year period prior to death, but he did not have the terminal exhaustion syndrome with high fever and coma. The day of death he became strangely quiet, although clear and responsive and not in a stupor or coma. He suddenly fainted and did not revive in spite of efforts to resuscitate him (Dynes, 1969, p. 26).

Dynes concluded his review by noting that we are far from an explanation of the phenomenon of sudden death.

It is interesting to note that Dynes described two types of sudden death, one following hyperactivity and the other following hypoactivity. These appear, on the surface at least, to correspond to the processes described by Cannon and Richter respectively. Perhaps many cases of sudden death are a result of excessive stimulation of the sympathetic or the parasympathetic systems.

Comment

Clearly, the ideas presented in this chapter are quite speculative. However, they serve to illustrate once more the many ways in which the autonomic nervous system has been related to human behaviors. Good research data to back up the ideas presented in this chapter are not presently available. However, the ideas presented in this chapter may serve to guide investigators in the future when they examine cases of voodoo death or sudden death. Investigators should look to see whether overstimulation of either the sympathetic or the parasympathetic systems has occurred. Furthermore, it may be that P-type individuals are more prone to voodoo death and sudden death from excessive parasympathetic activity whereas S-type individuals are more prone to voodoo death and sudden death from excessive sympathetic activity.

REFERENCES

Barber, T. X.: Death by suggestion. *Psychosom Med, 23*: 153-155, 1961.
Cannon, W.: Voodoo death. *Am Anthropol, 44*: 169-181, 1942.
Dynes, J.: Sudden death. *Dis Nerv Sys, 30*: 24-28, 1969.
Lester, D.: Voodoo death. *Am Anthropol, 74*: 386-390, 1972.
Richter, C.: On the phenomenon of sudden death in animals and men. *Psychom Med, 19*: 190-198, 1957.
Spencer, B., and Gillin, F. J.: *The Native Tribes Of Central Australia.* London, Macmillan, 1899.

CHAPTER 15 SUICIDE AND HOMICIDE

THE PERSON who kills himself has often been viewed as an unaggressive person. He is the sort who does not attack others, either physically or verbally, but instead inhibits his aggression and turns it inward upon himself in some self-destructive way.

This idea was first proposed by Freud (at least, in modern times; in fact, the notion that suicide results from aggression felt toward others which is turned against the self instead is clearly present, for example, in the plays of Sophocles). Freud outlined two stages in the development of suicidal behavior. First of all, emotional investment is withdrawn from a lost object of love and relocated in the ego, where the loved one is recreated as a permanent feature of the self, as a kind of ideal self. This is called identification of the ego with the abandoned object. The ego can kill itself if it can direct aggression that it feels toward some object in the external world toward itself. So, after identifying with the lost love-object, the ego can direct its aggressive impulses felt for that object toward the part of the ego that has identified with the object and, thence, kill itself.

Psychologists and sociologists have emphasized only the part of this formulation dealing with aggression turned inward upon the self, and they have ignored the role of prior loss. Suicide is thus seen as an act on inward-directed aggression to be contrasted with acts of outward-directed aggression such as homicide.

THE THEORY OF HENRY AND SHORT*

The major theorists who have developed this notion have been Henry and Short (1954). They assumed that the basic and primary target of aggression is another person rather than the self. They then attempted to identify the sociological and psychological bases of the legitimization of other-oriented aggression. What enables the child to develop so that his primary response to frustration, that of other-oriented aggression, is seen as legitimate, while other children develop

---

*This section is based on Lester (1968b).

[88]

in such a way that this primary response is inhibited and self-directed aggression becomes legitimate?

Sociologically, the strength of external restraint was seen as the primary basis for the legitimization of other-oriented aggression. When behavior is required to conform rigidly to the demands and expectations of others, the share of others in the responsibility for the consequences of the behavior increases, thereby legitimizing other-oriented aggression. When external restraints are weak, the self must bear the responsibility for the frustration generated, and other-oriented aggression fails to be legitimized.

Henry and Short found two psychological correlates of other-oriented aggression in people: low superego strength and low guilt, and a physiological response to stress similar to the effects of noradrenalin. This latter finding, of course, was made by Funkenstein and discussed above (see Chapter 8). King and Henry (in Henry and Short, 1954) found that the types of cardiovascular reaction experienced by male college students during experimentally-induced stress was related to the degree of the severity of the punishment meted out by the father to the student and by the relative roles of the mother and father in administering discipline.

Students whose fathers were more severe were more likely to have noradrenalin response to stress, as compared to students whose fathers were less severe. Those students who had dominant fathers (from the point of view of which parent disciplined the student) had noradrenalin responses to stress whereas those students who had dominant mothers had adrenalin responses to stress.

How do experiences with parents determine the ways in which aggression is expressed? When the source of nurturance and love also administers the punishment, then the primary response of the child to the frustration of punishment (that of striking out against the aggressor) will be inhibited, for the frustrating person (the punisher) is also the source of nurturance. To aggress against the punisher threatens the supply of nurturance. Thus, the child who is punished by the source of nurturance (in most families, the mother) will develop habits of inhibiting this primary other-oriented aggression.

Henry and Short also argued that experience of love-oriented punishment will lead to habits of inhibiting the primary response to frustration (that of aggressing against the frustrating person). If the person who punishes the child does so by threatening to withdraw love and nurturance, then the child cannot aggress against the punisher, since that will make the threatened loss of love and nurturance even more likely.

Thus, the child who develops into a murderer will be expected to have had a father who punished him while the mother remained a source of nurturance, and a father who used physical punishment rather than love-oriented punishment. A child who later becomes suicidal will be expected to have had a mother who punished him, in addition to providing nurturance and love, and who used love-oriented techniques of punishment rather than physical punishment.

EMPIRICAL STUDIES OF THE PERSONALITY OF SUICIDES AND MURDERERS

There have been few studies of the personality of suicides and murderers for those dimensions of personality relevant to the present theory. In addition, those studies that have been conducted are far from consistent.

Koller and Castanos (1968) compared alcoholics who had attempted suicide with alcoholics who had not and found no differences in scores on a test of extraversion. Colson (1972), comparing students who were nonsuicidal with students who had attempted or threatened suicide, found the suicidal students to be more introverted. Colson also found the suicidal students to be more sensitizing (as compared to repressing). In contrast to this latter finding, Eisenthal (1967) found no differences in the viewing time of suicidal and non-suicidal psychiatric patients for threatening and anxiety-provoking slides, and so Eisenthal concluded that suicidal persons were not different from controls in repressing-sensitizing.

McDowall *et al.* (1968) found that female-attempted suicides were more hysteroid than female psychiatric patients who had not attempted suicide on a test of obsessoid-hysteroid traits. The males did not differ. Vinoda (1966) was not able to replicate this result(while Murthy (1969) found that the more lethal female suicide attempters were more obsessoid than the less lethal female suicide attempters.

All in all, these results are most confusing.

Comment

Although the basic ideas proposed by Henry and Short (1954) have been criticized and modified (Lester, 1968a, 1968b, 1972, 1973), the importance of their theory for the present theory is that it illustrates that some theorists have extended the ideas of Funkenstein (discussed above in Chapter 8) to the extremes of directing anger outwards and inwards, that is to say, to homicide and suicide. Henry and Short have characterized the murder as showing a noradrenalin response to frustration while the suicide shows an adrenalin response to frustration.

A second point worthy of note is that Henry and Short see the noradrenalin response to frustration as primary. The natural response of infants to frustration is the noradrenalin response. If they are exposed to particular parental influences, then they may develop adrenalin responses to frustration. This agrees with the finding noted by Funkenstein (1955) that in infancy the adrenal medulla has more noradrenalin than adrenalin, but later adrenalin becomes dominant.

REFERENCES

Colson, C. E.: Neuroticism, extraversion, and repression-sensitization in suicidal college students. *Br J Soc Clin Psychol, 11*: 88-89, 1972.

Eisenthal, S.: Suicide and aggression. *Psychol Rep, 21*: 745-751, 1957.

Funkenstein, D.: The physiology of fear and anger. *Sci Am, 192(5)*: 74-80, 1955.

Henry, A. F., and Short, J. F.: *Suicide And Homicide*. New York, Free Press, 1954.

Koller, K. M., and Castanos, J. N.: Attempted suicide and alcoholism. *Med J Aust, 2*: 835-837, 1968.

Lester D.: Attempted suicide as a hostile act. *J Psychol, 68*: 243-248, 1968a.

Lester, D.: Henry and Short on suicide. *J Psychol, 70*: 179-186, 1968b.

Lester, D.: *Why People Kill Themselves*. Springfeld, Charles C Thomas, 1972.

Lester, D.: Suicide and internal-external orientation. *Psychology*, in press, 1973.

McDowall, A. W., Brooke, E. M., Freeman-Browne, D. L., and Robin, A. A.: Subsequent suicide in depressed in-patients. *Br J Psychiatr, 114*: 749-754, 1968.

Murthy, V. N.: Personality and the nature of suicide attempts. *Br J Psychiatr, 115*: 791-795, 1969.

Vinoda, K. S.: Personality characteristics of attempted suicide. *Br J Psychiatr, 112*: 1143-1150, 1966.

CHAPTER 16 PSYCHOSOMATIC DISORDERS

THE INTENT of this chapter is merely to suggest that some psychosomatic diseases might well be incorporated into the theory proposed in this book. Two mechanisms are possible. If the disease has a psychosomatic basis, then psychological factors (including the personality dimensions discussed in this book) might well facilitate the development of particular diseases. Alternatively, since a physiological basis has been proposed for these personality traits, disturbances in this physiological base might result directly in disease. The first example that will be discussed is that of smoking and lung cancer.

SMOKING AND LUNG CANCER

Lung cancer is associated with smoking tobacco and experiments have shown that tobacco smoke causes lung cancer. However, Petrie (1967) has noted that certain kinds of people tend to smoke more than others: reducers smoke more than augmenters (see Chapter 3). The reason proposed by Petrie for this is similar to that proposed earlier by Schubert (1965).

Schubert found that smokers obtained higher scores on the MMPI scale of psychopathic deviation and lower scores on the scale of social-introversion. An item analysis showed that smokers described themselves as bored and as thrill-seekers, as behaving in socially unacceptable ways, and as having masculine traits. Schubert characterized smokers as arousal seekers, seeking physiological arousal through the use of tobacco. Insofar as smokers are more extraverted than non-smokers, they would seem to be reducers (and hence S-types).

Support for these ideas comes from Hall et al. (1973). Hall et al. studied the evoked electrical potentials in the central nervous system to visual stimuli and found that, when habitual smokers gave up smoking, the evoked potentials decreased and when they resumed smoking the evoked potentials increased. These changes support the proposition that tobacco smoking increases arousal. Smoking was also found to selectively enhance the perception of weak stimuli. This

[92]

supports Petrie's hypothesis. If smoking enhances the perception of weak stimuli, smoking makes people act like augmenters. Thus, it would appear that, when not smoking, smokers are reducers.

Matarazzo and Saslow (1960) reviewed a number of studies of correlates of smoking behavior and their findings support the ideas proposed here. In general, smokers gain less weight (Lynn, 1948) and participate more in contact sports (Lilienfeld, 1959). Smokers have more driving accidents, otbain higher scores on the Taylor Manifest Anxiety Scale, are less suggestible on a body-sway test of suggestibility, have more psychosomatic problems, consume more coffee and alcohol, and are more extraverted (Eysenck *et al.*, 1960). With respect to the increased ingestion of coffee by smokers, Troemel et al. (1951) reported that nicotine increased the speed of dark adaptation, an effect which is counteracted by small doses of caffeine. Thus, smokers may drink more coffee in order to counteract the physiological effects of the nicotine. Males smoke more than females (but this finding may well be determined by cultural mores). There were no racial differences in smoking behavior reported.

In a long-term study of smokers (Heath, 1958) smokers were found to be viscerotonic (rather than cerebrotonic), to have decreased reflexes, to have a rapid respiratory rate, and to indulge in more sighs and swallowing.

Again, these conclusions support the proposition that smokers are S-type individuals. There is also a suspicion that smokers may be N subtypes rather than A subtypes since they gain less weight and participate in sports more. The finding that smokers are more viscerotonic whereas nonsmokers are more cerebrotonic (Heath, 1958) may merely be a reflection of the fact that extraversion is shown by both viscerotonics and somatotonics and so the two dimensions often seem similar (see Chapter 9). However, the classification of smokers as N subtypes must be regarded as less well validated than their assignment as S-types.

In conclusion, smokers are S-types. Since smokers are more likely to get lung cancer, we would expect to find an excess of S-types among lung cancer patients. To date, there have been few studies of cancer patients that bear upon the dimensions relevant to the theory proposed in this book. This is an old report that cancer patients were extraverted (Evans, 1926), a report that they tend to be endomorphic rather than ectomorphic (Sheldon, 1942), and a report by Kissen (1962) that males with lung cancer have a higher incidence of peptic ulcer and psychosomatic complaints in general.

These data support the notion that those who get lung cancer are S-type individuals, but the validity of this conclusion must await the collection of more complete data.

ASTHMA

Knapp (1969) has discussed the relationship of autonomic nervous system functioning to asthma. He noted that parasympathomimetic drugs (such as mecholyl) produce asthma-like responses, which are blocked by atropine. Vagal stimulation produces asthma-like responses, and again this effect can be blocked by atropine. Other investigators (for example, Mathe and Knapp, 1969) have stressed dysfunction of the sympathetic system. Mathe and Knapp argued that there is impaired mobilization of adrenalin in asthmatics, that is, when under stress, asthmatics do not become as sympathetically activated as normal individuals.

However, Knapp (1969) felt that the relative roles of the parasympathetic and the sympathetic systems in asthmatics were not completely clear yet since antimuscarinic agents (cholinergic depressants) have a relatively weak action in relieving bronchoconstriction and since Hahn (1966) has found evidence that asthmatic children appeared to have activated sympathetic systems when heart rate and skin temperature responses were studied.

Empirical data on the personality dimensions discussed in this book do not clarify the issue. Although Witkin (1965) reported that asthmatics were field dependent, Franks and Leigh (1959) found no differences between asthmatics and normals in the speed of conditioning in a classical conditioning task or in their extraversion scores on a psychological questionnaire.

PEPTIC ULCERS

In Chapter 2, chronic parasympathetic activation was suggested to be the basis for the development of peptic ulcers. Severing the vagus nerve (a cranial nerve) often leads to disappearance of the ulcer. Thus, it would seem reasonable to classify persons with peptic ulcers as P-types.

Maher (1966) described the personality of patients with peptic ulcers and noted their strong needs for affection and dependence. These needs are usually denied and the patient either acts ambitiously and assertively or else he behaves inhibitedly and unassertively while denying that he does so. Sarason (1972) described ulcer patients who were passive, shy, dependent, and anxious. Eberhard (1968) and Spiro (1971) have noted that peptic ulcer patients tended to be ectomorphs, which supports their classification as P-types. Furthermore, Spiro (1971) has noted that ulcer patients generally have low blood pressure.

On the other hand, Eberhard (1968) studied twins concordant and discordant for ulcers and found the ulcer twins to have a shorter duration of the spiral after-effect. This would make the ulcer patients extraverts (according to Eysenck [1965]) and thus S-types. Also, Petrie (1967) reported the case of a patient with a peptic ulcer who was found to be an extreme reducer (and so an S-type).* Eberhard found the ulcer twins to be less field dependent, while Witkin (1965) has reported that ulcer patients are more field dependent than comparison groups.

Thus, the evidence points both ways: peptic ulcer patients as P-types and as S-types. Perhaps systematic research would clarify this situation or, alternatively, we may find that there are two types of ulcer patients, one an S-type and one a P-type (perhaps corresponding to the two types described by Maher). In this respect, it has been reported that some patients with ulcers overeat (that is, are bulimic) while others undereat (that is, are anorexic).

Since the role of external stress factors plays so strong a part in the genesis of psychosomatic disorders, it may be that all kinds of individuals can be stressed sufficiently so that they respond with the development of peptic ulcers. Yet, it may still be that P-types are

---

*In contrast to this, Wolf and Goodell (1968) have reported that gastric hyperfunction (hyperemia and engorgement of gastric mucosa) is associated with lowered pain thresholds.

more susceptible to the development of peptic ulcers than S-types. Thus, peptic ulcer patients may contain a large group of P-type individuals and a smaller group of S-type individuals.

Comment

The notion that balance in the autonomic nervous system underlies many psychosomatic disorders has been developed by Gellhorn (1957). Gellhorn stressed that the response to a (stressful) stimulus by the autonomic nervous system may differ from individual to individual and, within any individual, from one time to another. Gellhorn and Loofbourrow (1963) have focussed upon the hypothalamus as the main center for regulating the balance between the sympathetic and the parasympathetic systems. The balance can be affected both by drugs and by external stimulation.

However, the relevance of the autonomic nervous system to the etiology of psychosomatic disorders is by no means as clear as in the case of the other psychopathological behaviors already discussed. Although many psychosomatic disorders are afflictions of parts of the body controlled by the autonomic nervous system, most investigators have focussed upon variables not closely related to the functioning of the autonomic nervous system. (Maher [1966] has provided a good perspective on representative research into psychosomatic disorders.) Thus, there is relatively little available data with which to explore the association of psychosomatic disorders with the theory proposed in this book.

REFERENCES

Eberhard, G.: Peptic ulcer in twins. *Acta Psychiatr Scand* [Supp] *205*: 1-118, 1968.

Evans, E.: *A Psychological Study Of Cancer.* New York, Dodd Mead, 1926.

Eysenck, H. J.: *Fact And Fiction In Psychology.* Baltimore, Penguin, 1965.

Eysenck, H. J., Tarrant, M., Woolf, M., and England, L.: Smoking and personality. *Br Med J, 1*: 1456-1460, 1960.

Franks, C. M., and Leigh, D.: The theoretical and experimental application of a conditioning model to a consideration of bronchial asthma in man. *J Psychosom Res, 4*: 88-98, 1959.

Gellhorn, E.: *Autonomic imbalance and the hypothalamus.* Minneapolis: University of Minnesota Press, 1957.

Gellhorn, E., and Loofbourrow, G. N.: *Emotions And Emotional Disorders.* New York, Hoeber, 1963.

Hahn, W.: Autonomic responses of asthmatic children. *Psychosom Med, 28*: 323-332, 1966.

Hall, R., Rappaport, M., Hopkins, H., and Griffin, R.: Tobacco and evoked potential. *Science, 180*: 212-214, 1973.

Heath, C. W.: Differences between smokers and nonsmokers. *Arch Intern Med, 101*: 377-388, 1958.

Kissen, D. M.: Relationships between primary lung cancer and peptic ulcer in males. *Psychosom Med, 24*: 133-147, 1962.

Knapp, P. H.: The asthmatic and his environment. *J Nerv Ment Dis, 149*: 133-151, 1969.

Lilienfeld, A. M.: Emotional and other selected characteristics of cigarette smokers and nonsmokers as related to epidemiological studies of lung cancer and other diseases. *J Nat Cancer Inst, 22*: 259-282, 1959.

Lynn, R. M.: A study of smokers and nonsmokers as related to achievement and various personal characteristics. *Univ North Carol Rec Res Progr, 464*: 164, 1948.

Maher, B.: *Principles Of Psychopathology.* New York, McGraw-Hill, 1966.

Matarazzo, J. D., and Saslow, G.: Psychological and related characteristics of smokers and nonsmokers. *Psychol Bull, 57*: 493-513, 1960.

Mathe, A., and Knapp, P. H.: A psychophysiological study of arousal in bronchial asthma. *Am Psychosom Assoc,* Cincinnati, 1969.

Petrie, A.: *Individuality In Pain and Suffering.* Chicago, University of Chicago Press, 1967.

Sarason, I. G.: *Abnormal Psychology.* New York, Appleton-Century-Crofts, 1972.

Schubert, D. S.: Arousal seeking as a central factor in tobacco smoking. *Int J Soc Psychiatr, 11*: 221-225, 1955.

Sheldon, W. H.: *The varieties of temperament.* New York: Harper, 1942.

Spiro, H. M.: *Peptic Ulcer.* Fort Washington, William Rorer, 1971.

Troemel, R. G., Davis, R. T., and Hendley, C. D.: Dark adaptation as a function of caffeine and nicotine administration. *Proc South Dak Acad Sci, 30*: 79-84, 1951.

Witkin, H.: Psychological differentiation and forms of pathology. *J Abnorm Psychol, 70*: 317-336, 1965.

Wolf, S., and Goodell, H.: *Stress And Disease.* Springfield, Charles C Thomas, 1968.

CHAPTER 17

ANXIETY AND NATIONAL DIFFERENCES

A STUDY OF research that has been conducted into anxiety indicates that anxiety is a very broad term and is assessed in a variety of ways by different investigators (Levitt, 1967). The physiological measures of anxiety are very similar, if not identical, to the measures used to assess the balance of the autonomic nervous system. In some studies on anxiety, those concerned with the current state of the individual, these measures are used to tap transient changes in the body. In other studies, those concerned with anxiety proneness, the measures are used to tap chronic states and these measures resemble greatly those used in studies of autonomic nervous system balance.

Psychological measures of anxiety are extremely varied and the many measures may not all be tapping the same dimension. For example, the Manifest Anxiety Scale (Taylor, 1953) has been conceptualized by Gray (1971; see Chapter 4) as measuring a dimension whose poles might be characterized as neurotic introversion and stable extraversion. If this notion has any validity then this particular measure of anxiety is related to extraversion which we have related to the balance in the autonomic nervous system.

It does not seem profitable here to review work on anxiety in general. Much of it would not be relevant to the present theory. However, it is worthwhile to consider a particular study of anxiety by Lynn (1971) since Lynn uses a concept of anxiety that resembles quite closely the personality dimensions relevant to the present theory, and since Lynn uses the concept of anxiety to speculate upon and provide evidence for national differences in personality. Thus, Lynn's work serves to suggest that the present theory too could be extended to account for national differences in personality.

NATIONAL DIFFERENCE IN ANXIETY

Lynn (1971) has conducted a study on national character that is based upon an underlying trait of anxiety and which is relevant to the present theory. Lynn started from the fact that, in a sample of 18 developed nations, high rates of mental illness were associated with high calorie intake, low rates of suicide, and low rates of alcoholism (as assessed from the death rate from cirrhosis of the liver). Lynn considered what general factor might underlie this matrix of inter-correlations. The degree of affluence and the degree of urbanization in the nations did not appear to be highly related to the four basic variables, and Lynn advanced the hypothesis that the correlations were due to the level of anxiety in the sample of nations. Nations with a high level of anxiety would have, in this view, high suicide rates, high rates of alcoholism, low rates for the incidence of mental illness, and low rates of calorie intake.

A critical factor here is what is meant by anxiety. Lynn is rather diffuse in this respect. His definition of what is anxiety includes measures from psychological questionnaires (and he sees anxiety as a higher order factor in Eysenck's theory [Eysenck, 1964], principally a function of neuroticism but also to a lesser extent a function of introversion), measures of the reactivity of the sympathetic system, and cortical arousal. These different definitions may well be of very different variables, and so not equivalent. For example, in Chapter 4 it was argued that sympathetic arousal was related to extraversion. Thus, to include both sympathetic arousal and introversion in one's definition of anxiety is, from the point of view of the present theory, erroneous.

Be this as it may, it is of interest to review Lynn's justification for relating his four basic national variables (suicide, mental illness, alcoholism, and calorie intake) to anxiety.

(1) Mental illness:

Lynn saw mental illness, which he measured by noting the number of hospitalized psychiatric patients, as synonymous with psychosis. To demonstrate that psychotics were characterized, on the whole, by low anxiety, Lynn noted that measures of sympathetic system activity and reactivity indicated low arousal and reactivity in psychotics. The success of electro-convulsive therapy and a variety of drugs (such as Iproniazid, imipramine, and nitrogen inhalation) was seen as supporting evidence, since these procedures increase sympathetic system activity. The fact that sympathetic system activity declines with age was seen to be consistent with the increase in the incidence of psychosis among older people.

The poorer performance of psychotics in classical conditioning tasks, the low rates of excretion of 17-ketosteroids in the urine of psychotics, the low rate of steroid excretion, the subnormal response of the adrenal cortex to the adrenocorticotrophic hormone (ACTH), and the low rates of hippuric acid secretion, were all seen as validating the assumption that psychotics were low in anxiety.

Lynn noted that a small group of psychotics (acute and paranoid cases) and some other psychiatric disorders (such as anxiety neuroses) were characterized by high sympathetic system reactivity. However, these patients make up only a small proportion of hospitalized psychiatric patients.

(2) Suicide:

Lynn's evidence relating suicide to anxiety is quite poor. The only empirical data that he could report was a study indicating that attempted suicides received higher anxiety scores on a questionnaire test of anxiety than the general population. Furthermore, Lynn was forced to explain the negative association between rates of mental illness and the rates of suicide over his sample of nations, when it is well documented that the incidence of suicide is higher in those with psychiatric illness than in those with no psychiatric illness. Lynn speculates that it is only the highly anxious psychiatric patients that complete suicide, a possible though unlikely assumption.

(3) Caloric Intake:

Lynn argued that anxiety reduced eating behavior since the sympathetic system activity that is characteristic of anxiety inhibits digestion. Lynn noted the common use of amphetamines (an adrenergic drug) to suppress appetite. He also noted that pre-frontal leucotomy reduced anxiety and increased appetite, so that patients who have had this operation generally become overweight.

(4) Alcoholism:

Lynn argued that alcohol reduced anxiety, based upon its depressant effect on the nervous system. He noted that studies of animals (Masserman and Yum, 1946) and primitive societies (Horton, 1943) indicated that when subjected to psychological stress the intake of alcohol was increased.

Lynn validated his notion that his four national variables measured anxiety by correlating them with anxiety scores of representative samples of students in the nations that he studied. The correlations were in the expected directions: high anxiety in the college students of a nation was associated with high suicide and alcoholism rates and low mental illness rates and calorific intake.

To obtain one measure of anxiety for each of the nations in his sample, Lynn ranked each nation for each of the four national variables, summed these ranks for each nation, and then re-ranked his nations for their score on this latter measure. Lynn explored the association between this composite measure of anxiety and other national variables.

(1) Accident Proneness: Lynn found that there were more deaths from motor vehicle accidents in countries with high levels of anxiety. Lynn noted that high levels of anxiety impair motor performance and felt that this fact explained the association. (It might be noted that a good deal of research indicates that moderate anxiety improves performance on a variety of tasks [e.g. Hebb, 1955].) Lynn noted that accident prone individuals were generally extraverted (but from his point of view anxiety and extraversion are independent factors. From the point of view of the present theory they are similar if assessed appropriately).

(2) Deaths From Atherosclerosis And Coronary Heart Disease: Lynn found that nations with high levels of anxiety had low rates of death from atherosclerosis and coronary heart disease. Lynn's review of the literature indicated that there was no clear data to indicate the existence of a "coronary personality." There was data, however, to indicate that coronory patients were overweight.

(3) Deaths From Duodenal Ulcers And Hypertension: Lynn found that deaths from ulcers and hypertension were not related to national anxiety levels. With respect to ulcers, Lynn reviewed opinions suggesting that ulcers were due to parasympathetic system activity and not sympathetic system activity. Lynn implied that these two systems

of activity operate independently, which is by no means proven or even likely. It would seem that ulcer patients should have low levels of sympathetic system activity and thus low levels of anxiety.

There appears to be no relationship between hypertension and anxiety as measured by psychological questionnaires. On the other hand, hypertension does appear to be associated with sympathetic system arousal.

Lynn noted that deaths from ulcers and deaths from hypertension were associated over samples of nations, and he considered the possibility that these death rates assessed national levels of anxiety rather than the four national variables that he had proposed. Lynn felt that the evidence supporting the validity of his four measures was better than that supporting the validity of the death rates from ulcers and hypertension. Lynn also considered the possibility that the death rates from ulcers and hypertension measured a national trait of extraversion. Although hypertension patients appear to be hostile or to have repressed hostile impulses, ulcer patients appear to be introverted (Kanter and Hazelton, 1964). Lynn correlated the death rates from ulcers and hypertension with national scores on a test of extraversion for a sample of nations and found negative but nonsignificant correlations. Lynn concluded that death rates from hypertension and ulcers measured some national trait, but that it was far from clear what that trait was.

(It is worth repeating here that Lynn saw anxiety as very different from extraversion-introversion, whereas the theory proposed in this book would see extraversion-introversion as a similar variable to some measures of anxiety.)

(4) Tobacco Consumption: Lynn found that nations with high anxiety levels consumed much less tobacco than nations with low levels of anxiety. Lynn reviewed research indicating that smokers are more extraverted (and he confirmed this by correlating the two variables over a sample of nations). Although smokers and nonsmokers did not appear to differ in tests of anxiety, Lynn felt that nicotine was a stimulant and thus raises anxiety as defined by Lynn. Lynn argued that, therefore, only those with low anxiety levels would smoke, since only these people would need to raise their level of anxiety.

(5) Sex and Celibacy: Lynn argued that high levels of anxiety would inhibit sexual behavior. However, the associations between national anxiety levels and measures of the extent of premarital sexual intercourse and the extent of celibacy for men and for women proved to be nonsignificant.

(6) Economic Growth: Nations with high levels of anxiety had significantly higher rates of economic growth. Lynn's review of the literature seemed to indicate that there was no association between anxiety levels and achievement motivation. Lynn argued that the reasons why highly anxious nations grew faster economically were (a) that highly anxious people work harder (Lynn ignored that possibility that their increased accident proneness will cause them to make more errors), and (b) that high levels of anxiety increase the chances of a person being creative. Lynn (1969) has found that entrepreneurs tend to have high levels of neuroticism (which for Lynn assesses anxiety levels) and so Lynn argued that high levels of anxiety lead to more creative persons in the society, which leads to more entrepreneurs, which leads to faster economic growth.

Lynn postulated the existence of two factors that lead to different levels of anxiety in different nations. The first was climate. Lynn found that hot summers and a high incidence of thunderstorms were associated with high levels of national anxiety. Lynn noted that suicide rates and beer consumption rose in the summer, while calorie intake dropped. There was no data available to explore seasonal variations in chronic psychosis. Lynn noted, in addition, that the summer rise in suicide rates was more marked in nations with high levels of anxiety than in nations with low levels of anxiety. Lynn reviewed research indicating that body temperature was associated with sympathetim system arousal and he suggested that body temperature might be a good measure of anxiety. Lynn also argued that thunderstorm activity lead to heightened sympathetic system arousal (Huntington, 1945).

A second factor that Lynn proposed to account for national differences in anxiety levels was race. In Europe, Lynn took the division by Coons (1939) of peoples in Europe into nine races. On the basis of his data, Lynn proposed that there are four high-anxiety races (Nordic,

Dinaric, Alpine, and Borreby) and two low-anxiety races (Nordic and Brünn). If this is true, then the national differences in anxiety levels can be predicted on the basis of their racial composition.

Comment

A couple of comments are important to note here. First, it is note-worthy that Lynn attempted to justify the associations that he found from ecological correlations over nations by reviewing data on indi-viduals. Ecological correlations may be very differently determined from associations between behaviors correlated over individuals (Lester, 1971).

Secondly, from the point of view of the present book, Lynn's work is difficult to review tidily. Lynn's basic dimension in that of anxiety, which he identifies with sympathetic system activation. However, in Chapter 4 above, sympathetic system predominance was associated with extraversion. Yet, Lynn sees extraversion as a dimension inde-pendent of anxiety. Instead, he identifies anxiety with neuroticism. Thus, a comparison of Lynn's ideas with those of the present book tends to become confusing at times.

Despite this, a translation of Lynn's ideas into the language of the present book shows that a good deal of Lynn's work supports the ideas expressed here. Furthermore, it shows how the ideas expressed in this book may easily be extended to a study of national character.

REFERENCES

Coons, C. S.: *The Races Of Europe.* New York, Macmillan, 1939.

Eysenck, H. J.: *Crime And Personality.* Boston, Houghton-Mifflin, 1964.

Gray, J.: *The Psychology Of Fear And Stress.* New York, McGraw-Hill, 1971.

Hebb, D. O.: Drives and the cns. *Psychol Rev, 62:* 243-254, 1955.

Horton, D.: The functions of alcohol in primitive societies. *Q J Studies Alc, 4:* 199-220, 1943.

Huntington, E.: *Mainsprings Of Civilization.* New York, Wiley, 1945.

Kanter, V. B., and Hazelton, J. E.: An attempt to measure some aspects of personality in young men with duodenal ulcers by means of questionnaires and a projective tests. *J Psychosom Res, 8:* 297-309, 1964.

Lester, D.: Suicide and homicide. *Soc Psychiatr, 6:* 80-82, 1971.

Levitt, E. E.: *The Psychology Of Anxiety.* Indianapolis, Bobbs-Merrill, 1967.

Lynn, R.: Personality characteristics of a group of entrepreneurs. *Occup Psychol, 43:* 151-152, 1969.

Lynn, R.: *Personality And National Character.* New York, Pergamon, 1971.

Masserman, J., and Yum, K. S.: An analysis of the influence of alcohol on experimental neurosis in cats. *Psychosom Med, 8:* 36-52, 1946.

Taylor, J. A.: A personality scale of manifest anxiety. *J Abnorm Soc Psychol, 48:* 285-290, 1953.

PART FIVE   **SEX DIFFERENCES IN BEHAVIOR**

SEX DIFFERENCES IN PERCEPTUAL AND MOTOR FUNCTIONING

CHAPTER 18

B ROVERMAN *et al.* (1968) have argued that sex differences in cognitive abilities reflect sex-related differences in physiology. Females are found to surpass males on simple, overlearned perceptual-motor tasks whereas males are found to excel on more complex tasks requiring an inhibition of immediate responses to obvious stimulus attributes in favor of responses to less obvious stimulus attributes. Broverman *et al.* argued that these sex differences were reflections of differences in the balance between the adrenergic activating and the cholinergic inhibitory neural processes. (I would rather prefer a statement of this difference in terms of the balance between the sympathetic and the parasympathetic systems.) These differences in the autonomic nervous system were in turn seen as dependent upon the sex homones.

In general, it is found that females do better at tasks which (1) are based on past experience rather than problem solving, (2) involve minimal mediation by higher cognitive processes, (3) involve fine coordinations of small muscles with perceptual and attentional processes, and (4) are evaluated in terms of speed and accuracy of repetitive responses. These tasks include speed of naming colors, speed of canceling numbers, reading speed, coding speed, tapping speed, writing speed, walking, typing, simple calculations, eye-blink conditioning, discrimination of letter series, letter canceling, auditory pitch discrimination, visual acuity, and critical flicker fusion.

Males do better at tasks which (1) involve inhibition or delay of initial responses to obvious stimulus attributes in favor of responses to less obvious stimulus attributes, (2) involve extensive mediation of higher cognitive processes as opposed to automatic or reflexive stimulus response connections, and (3) are evaluated in terms of the production of solutions to novel tasks or situations. These tasks include temporal judgment with delayed responding, mirror tracing, maze performance, ability to retard overpracticed motor movements, dis-

[109]

criminant reaction time, and reversal of habits (such as counting backwards).

Although the usual explanation for these differences is based on differences in the ways that boys and girls are raised and the activities for which they are rewarded, Broverman *et al.* noted that such an explanation could not account for female superiority in such tasks as eye-blink conditioning and acuity in sensory thresholds such as hearing; nor could it account for sex differences in lower animals where, for example, male rats learn mazes faster than female rats whereas female rats are superior in running wheels (which require excellent coordination of small muscles with perceptual functioning).

Broverman *et al.* noted that the sympathetic system has a mobilizing function and prepares the organism for action. It controls motor activity, sensory reactivity, wakefulness, and alertness. On the other hand, the parasympathetic system works toward protection, conservation, and relaxation of the organism when action is not required. It promotes sleep, inhibition of activity, and relaxation.

Broverman *et al.* hypothesized that the sympathetic system facilitates performance of simple perceptual-motor tasks whereas the parasympathetic system facilitates performance at tasks in which inhibition of immediate responding is required, together with restructuring of the perceived stimuli. They tested this hypothesis by reviewing the research conducted using drugs that affect the adrenergic and cholinergic systems to explore the effects of these drugs on perceptual-motor functioning. On the whole, the research reviewed supported their hypotheses. For example, the sympathomimetic drug amphetamine has been found to improve performance at tasks such as canceling numbers and visual acuity; and adrenalin (also a sympathomimetic drug) has been found to impair performance at the task of writing slowly. In contrast, sympatholytic drugs (which depress adrenergic functioning), such as chlorpromazine, slow performance at tapping speed tasks and impair flicker fusion, while reducing impulsive and careless errors in maze learning.

Drugs which stimulate the parasympathetic system, such as eserine and acetylcholine, impair motor activity when injected into animals while improving the ability of the animals to learn mazes. Parasympatholytic drugs (that is, anticholinergic drugs) such as atropine and scopolamine increase motor activity in animals while impairing their ability to learn mazes.

For the final link in their chain of reasoning, Broverman *et al.* argued that estrogens (the female sex hormone) tend to increase the activity of the sympathetic system. They noted that androgens (the male sex hormone) appeared also to have an activating effect on the sympathetic system, but they argued that the effect of androgens was much smaller than the effect of estrogens. For example, they noted that estrogens inhibit the activity of choline acetylase (see Chapter 12) in the rat hypothalamus while androgens do not.

To sum up, therefore, Broverman *et al.* have argued that the female sex hormone leads to a greater predominance of the sympathetic system in females as compared to males, and that this psysiological difference can adequately account for sex differences in perceptual-motor functioning.

This theory proposed by Broverman *et al.* is congruent with a theory proposed by Lester (1967, 1968) to account for sex differences in exploratory behavior in rats. Lester proposed a theory that postulated that female rats had a higher base level of fear than male rats, and that this difference could account for observed sex differences in exploratory behavior. Lester (1968) modified this theory by noting that fear was but one contributor to the arousal level of an organism. Thus, Lester's new theory was that female rats had a higher level of arousal than male rats. Although Lester did not comment on the relevance of the dimensions of fear and arousal to the autonomic nervous system, it is clear that the dimensions are related to sympathetic system predominance. Thus, Lester's theory of exploratory behavior is derivable from the theory of Broverman *et al.*

Comment

This chapter has made two noteworthy contributions to the development of the theory in this book. First, the theory has been extended to sex differences in behavior, and in the following chapter we will explore whether the theory can explain sex differences in personality and psychopathology in addition to sex differences in perceptual-motor functioning. Secondly, the theory has now been applied to theories of animal behavior, and in particular the behavior of rats. It thus appears that the theory might generalize to a variety of species.

REFERENCES

Broverman, D. M., Klaiber, E. L., Kobayashi, Y., and Vogel, W.: Roles of activation and inhibition in sex differences in cognitive abilites. *Psychol Rev, 75*: 23-50, 1968.
Lester, D.: Sex differences in exploration. *Psychol Rec, 17*: 55-62, 1967.
Lester, D.: The effect of fear and anxiety on exploration. *J Gen Psychol, 79*: 105-120, 1968.

CHAPTER 19 SEX DIFFERENCES IN PERSONALITY AND PSYCHOPATHOLOGY

IN THE PREVIOUS CHAPTER, it was argued that an examination of the perceptual-cognitive functioning of males and females suggested the possibility that females have a lesser degree of parasympathetic activation than do males. It is of interest to inquire whether this hypothesis is supported by data from personality tests and psychopathology.

No studies of sex differences in reducing-augmenting have been reported. With respect to extraversion-introversion, Anastasi (1958) analysed the norms for the Bernreuter Personality Inventory and found that females obtained higher introversion scores than males (thus making them P-types). However, the sexes did not differ in sociability. Females have been reported to be field-dependent than males (Long, 1972). According to the present author, this would make females S-types, but as noted in Chapter 6, others (e.g. Long, 1972) see field-dependent people as P-types. Furthermore, methodology in rod-and-frame research is poor and a number of well carried out studies report no sex differences in field-dependence (e.g. Lester, 1971).

Schwartz (1972) has reported upon the repression-sensitization scores of some 50,000 medical patients and he found that females were significantly more sensitizing than males at all ages. (Incidentally, younger patients were significantly more sensitizing than older patients.) According to the categorization of repression-sensitization with respect to the present theory, this would indicate that females are P-types whereas males are S-types.

No studies of sex differences in the physiological response to stress (see Chapter 8) have been reported. On Sheldon's constitutional typology, females are found to be more endomorphic (Bardwick, 1971) suggesting that they are S-types, subtype A.

Females are less often found to be alcoholics (P-types) than males and less often found to be delinquents (S-types). Females are found to be more often neurotic and less often psychotic than males (Lester, 1970), but from Chapters 12 and 13 it can be seen these broad diagnostic categories are quite heterogeneous. With respect to suicide and homicide (which are both S-type behaviors), males have much higher rates of both. Thus, perhaps it might be argued that females are P-types. However, proportionately, females are more suicidal than homicidal as compared to males and, so we might argue that females have a tendency to be S-types, subtype A.

It might be noted here that those with hysterical neuroses tend to be predominantly female whereas delinquents tend to be predominantly male. It has been noted that these two behaviors (hysterical neurosis and delinquency) appear to have a similar etiology but that the etiological factors lead to different behavioral manifestations in males and females (Templer and Lester, in press; see Chapter 13). Thus, it becomes difficult to classify males and females simply on the basis of these behaviors. It may be that the variables that lead to delinquency in males and hysterical neuroses in females are related to the subtype (A or N) of their predominant sympathetic activation.

In conclusion, there is some data to indicate that females are P-types but there are also data to indicate that they are S-types subtype A. These conclusions may well be resolved by more adequate research into the relevant personality and psychopathological traits. Alternatively, the differences may not be incompatible. It may be that females tend more to parasympathetic predominance but the sex differences may be small. This will mean that a large proportion (though not perhaps a majority) of females will have sympathetic predominance and these females may be A subtypes rather than N subtypes.

Clearly, however, resolution of these questions must await further research.

REFERENCES

Anastasi, A.: *Differential Psychology.* New York, Macmillan, 1958.

Bardwick, J.: *The Psychology Of Women.* New York, Harper and Row, 1971.

Lester, D.: Suicidal behavior, sex, and mental disorder. *Psychol Rep, 27:* 61-62, 1970.

Lester, G.: Subjects' assumptions and scores on the rod-and-frame test. *Percept Mot Skills, 32:* 205-206, 1971.

Long, G.: *Field Dependency-Independency.* Pensacola, Naval Aerospace Medical Research Laboratory, 1972.

Schwartz, M. S.: The repression-sensitization scale. *J Clin Psychol,* *28*: 72-73, 1972.

Templer, D., and Lester, D.: Conversion disorders. In press, 1973.

PART SIX **CONCLUSIONS**

CHAPTER 20 CONCLUSIONS

THE THEORY proposed in this book is that there are three major response patterns of the autonomic nervous system: parasympathetic (P-type), sympathetic with noradrenalin activation (S-type subtype N), and sympathetic with adrenalin activation (S-type subtype A). Individuals differ with respect to which of these response patterns predominates and with respect to the sensitivity (or threshold to arousal) of these response patterns.

It has been proposed here that many personality dimensions fit into this typology. For example, Petrie's (1967) notion of reducing-augmenting and Eysenck's (1964) notion of extraversion-introversion fit easily into the schema: reducers and extraverts are S-types while augmenters and introverts are P-types.

Sheldon's constitutional theory of personality was seen to fit simply into the typology and, in addition, many behavior disorders (such as delinquency, alcoholism, and schizophrenia) were also found to fit into the typology. Furthermore sexual differences in behavior were found to be possibly related to the typology.

Several comments are worth making in conclusion. First it is noteworthy how many investigators have come to the conclusion that the behavior which they were studying might be related to the balance of the autonomic nervous system. I have not attempted to be exhaustive in my citing of authors who have suggested the influence of the autonomic nervous system but, even so, the number of authors cited is remarkable.

Secondly, I have not meant to imply that the research data unanimously supports my ideas. They clearly do not. My aim has been to outline a theory and adduce support for it. I am aware that each of the studies and theories I have cited has been subjected to much criticism. Eysenck's ideas on extraversion-introversion have received widespread comment, rod-and-frame studies are perhaps notoriously poor (from a methodological point of view), Broverman's theory of the cause of sexual differences in perceptual-cognitive functioning

(Broverman *et al.*, 1968) has been attacked (Parle, 1971), and so on.

However, despite these criticisms (which in fact accompany all heuristic research), the literature cited begins to build into a coherent framework. Should the edifice eventually be constructed be sound enough, its stability may transcend these individual criticisms.

THE CONSISTENCY OF THE EVIDENCE

As I noted above, the data that I have presented in this book has not been uniformly supportive of the predicted associations. There are a couple of reasons that might be suggested for this.

First of all, the theory does not propose three comparable types. Rather it proposes two types and then splits one of the types into two subtypes. This has implications for the success of predictions. For example, consider the prediction that extraverts are S-types while introverts are P-types. If a group of subjects is classified for the balance of their autonomic nervous systems and separately for their degree of extraversion-introversion, the predicted association might be less than perfect because of the existence of two kinds of S-types. Perhaps the particular test of extraversion being used taps a particular kind of extraversion. Such a possibility was noted in Chapter 4, where it was noted that extraversion involves two traits, sociability and impulsiveness. It was noted that British and American tests of extraversion differ with respect to the emphasis they place on each of these two traits of extraversion. This might mean in the hypothetical study that the P-types and the S-types subtype A might provide data in congruence with the prediction, but the data from the S-types subtype N might not, thereby reducing the magnitude of the correlation.

Secondly, the predictions made in this book involve personality traits and psychopathological behaviors which require operational definitions. These operational definitions may not be perfectly valid measures of the behavior under consideration. There are many psychological tests that claim to measure extraversion and the correlations between them are far from perfect. The diagnosis of schizophrenic or psychopath is by no means easy to make reliably or validly. The poor reliability and validity of the operational definitions of the variables crucial to the proposed theory may, therefore, account in part for the lack of consistency of the evidence adduced to support the theory.

THE SIMPLICITY OF THE PROPOSED THEORY

The simplicity of the theory proposed in this book is perhaps misleading. The theory can be made more complex and it is worthwhile to document several ways in which this can be done.

(1) In general, the theory presented here has taken the balance of the autonomic nervous system to be the fundamental physiological basis for personality. Is the balance of the subject in a resting state toward the sympathetic or toward the parasympathetic response pattern? Rubin (1962), in contrast, treated the two systems as independent. He categorized subjects for their sympathetic and parasympathetic functioning separately. By classifying each system independently and by categorizing each system in each subject as overactivated, normally activated, and underactivated, he was able to classify subjects into a three-by-three matrix, giving nine types of individuals (for example, normally activated sympathetic system and overactivated parasympathetic system, overactivated sympathetic system and underactivated parasympathetic system, and so on).

(2) It should also be noted that, although the distinction into sympathetic and parasympathetic predominance is clear from a conceptual point of view, biochemically the distinction is difficult to tease out. For example, although ultimately investigation of the theory proposed here would involve selective inhibition and excitation of the sympathetic and parasympathetic systems, this is not easy biochemically. The sympathetic system is both adrenergic and cholinergic while the parasympathetic system is cholinergic. Thus, cholinergic drugs, for example, interfer with both sympathetic and parasympathetic functioning.

Although I have stated the theory in terms of sympathetic versus parasympathetic predominance, it is possible to state the theory in terms of adrenergic-cholinergic functioning. Indeed, Rubin (1962) in discussing the influence of the autonomic nervous system in schizophrenia used a adrenergic-cholinergic categorization (see Chapter 12).

The method of stating the theory may have important implications for the deductions possible from the theory and for the particular methods used to test the theory.

(3) I have talked of the sympathetic and parasympathetic systems as if they were independent and linear. I noted in Chapter 2 that the two systems were not independent and that activation of one

system often resulted in activation of the other system. For example, as Arnold (1960) has noted, adrenalin in weak concentration improves the action of acetylcholine whereas in strong concentration it depresses the action of acetylcholine. On the other hand, noradrenalin has no effect on the action of acetylcholine (Burn, 1945).

Furthermore, it may be that the activation of either system is not linear, that is, that increasing degrees of activation of say the sympathetic system may not have linear or monotonic effects on a behavior trait under investigation.

(4) The majority of physiological investigations of the balance in the autonomic nervous system have measured peripheral physiological responses. However, some studies of autonomic arousal have utilized central measures (such as cortical arousal). Similarly, while the majority of the discussions of the involvement of the autonomic nervous system in behavior have focused upon the peripheral system, some discussions have focused upon the concentration of the neurohumors in the central nervous system. Personally, I see the peripheral system as critical to the theory proposed here, but the involvement of the central nervous system cannot, of course, be ruled out.

(5) Should the involvement of the central nervous system eventually be documented, it should be borne in mind that there are a good number of neurohumors operating in the central nervous system. In addition to noradrenalin, adrenalin, and acetylcholine, investigators have identified dopamine, serotonin, gamma-amino-butyric acid, and glutamic acid. To focus on just three of these neurohumors may be an oversimplification.

(6) The present theory has focused upon the balance of the autonomic nervous system. The autonomic nervous system may be categorized for other characteristics. Long (1972) noted that the *stability* of autonomic nervous system functioning may have important consequences for behavior, in addition to the *level of arousal*.

(7) Maher (1966) has suggested that the balance in the autonomic nervous system may be affected by learning (and experiential factors) as well as being affected by innate factors. The possibilities that learning may modify the autonomic nervous system balance allows for a much more complex theory.

THE PERVASIVENESS OF THE THEORY

The theory proposed in this book has enormous implications for behavior for the autonomic nervous system is involved in so many aspects of our behavior. Autonomic functioning is affected by a wide variety of drugs (including marihuana and alcohol [Ng *et al.*, 1973]) and by a wide variety of externally-derived stimuli. Thus, the theory permits many predictions to be made about short-term transient changes in behavior as well as making predictions about long-term stable personality functioning.

This reflects a general advantage of theories of behavior and personality based upon physiological processes. If the physiological processes are capable of both short-term and long-term changes, then the psychological theory based upon these physiological processes can also make predictions about short-term and long-term behavior.

Concluding Comment

In conclusion, the aim of the theory proposed here has been to synthesize a number of disparate categories and theories of personality and psychopathological functioning. In addition, the theory can be seen to generate an immense number of testable hypotheses about the associations between these aspects of function and about the underlying causes of them. The success of the theory will ultimately be measured by the research that it generates and by the results of this research.

REFERENCES

Arnold, M. B.: *Emotions And Personality*. New York, Columbia University Press, 1960.

Broverman, D., Klaiber, E., Kobayashi, Y., and Vogel, W.: Roles of activation and inhibition in sex differences in cognitive abilities. *Psychol Rev, 75:* 23-50, 1968.

Burn, J. H.: Relation of adrenaline to acetylcholine in the nervous system. *Physiol Rev, 25:* 377-394, 1945.

Eysenck, H. J.: *Crime And Personality*. Boston, Houghton Mifflin, 1964.

Long, G.: *Field dependency-independency*. Pensacola: Naval Aerospace Medical Research Laboratory, 1972.

Maher, B.: *Principles Of Psychopathology*. New York, McGraw-Hill, 1966.

Ng, L., Lamprecht, F., Williams, R., and Kopin, I.: $\triangle^9$-tetrahydrocannabinol and ethanol. *Science, 180*: 1368-1369, 1973.

Parlee, M.: Comment on Broverman et al. *Psychol Rev, 79*: 180-184, 1972.

Petrie, A.: *Individuality In Pain And Suffering*. Chicago, University of Chicago Press, 1967.

Rubin, L.: Patterns of adrenergic-cholinergic balance in the functional psychoses. *Psychol Rev, 69*: 501-519, 1962.

Sheldon, W. H.: *The Varieties Of Temperament*. New York, Harper, 1942.

NAME INDEX

A

Addus. H., 57
Alfert, E., 27-28
Anastasi, A., 113-114
Appley, M., 36
Arnold, M., 122-123
Averill, J., 46
Axelrod, J., 80

B

Badia, P., 28
Balint, M., 38, 41
Barber, T., 84, 87
Bardwick, J., 113-114
Beck, A., 46, 76, 78
Belmont, I., 41
Bergman, P., 68, 78
Bergquist, W., 28
Bevan, W., 80
Bexton, W., 70, 78
Birch, H., 40-41
Blackmore, W., 80
Blake, R., 41
Blaurock, M., 80
Bogdonoff, M., 36-37
Bowen, M., 61, 66
Bradley, C., 61, 66
Brelje, T., 28
Brody, N., 20, 22, 25
Brooke, E., 91
Broverman, D., 11-12, 33, 36, 75, 78, 109, 112, 119, 123
Bryan, J., 70, 79
Burn, J., 122-123
Buss, A., 72, 79
Byers, L., 79
Byrne, D., 27-28, 70

C

Callaway, E., 18-19, 32, 36, 40-41
Cameron, N., 71, 79

Cantwell, D., 83
Cannon, W., 84, 87
Carrigan, P., 23, 25
Castanos, J., 90-91
Cattell, R., 23, 38, 41
Chess, S., 55, 57
Claridge, G., 22, 25
Cleghorn, R., 79
Cohen, A., 31, 36
Cohen, S., 36-37
Coleman, J., 56-57
Colson, C., 90-91
Conners, C., 66
Conrad, K., 50-51
Coons, C., 103-104
Cortes, J., 49, 51, 65-66
Coventry, J., 31, 37
Cowen, E., 55, 57
Crookes, T., 79
Curtis, G., 77, 79
Cutts, K., 61, 66

D

Darrow, C., 80
Davis, R., 97
Dembo, D., 40-41
Denison, M., 57
Drolette, M., 47
Du Preeze, P., 31, 36
Dynes, J., 86-87

E

Eberhard, G., 95-96
Edwards, A., 50-51
Eisenberg, L., 61, 66
Eisenthal, S., 90-91
England, L., 96
Epps, P., 65-66
Escalona, S., 68, 78
Evans, E., 94, 96
Evans, F., 31, 36
Eysenck, H., 8, 15, 18, 20, 25, 31, 34,

SUBJECT INDEX

A

Accident proness, 101, 103
Acuity, 110
Age, 30, 40, 50, 77
Aggression, 88
Alcohol, 18, 93, 123
Alcoholism, 17, 32, 55, 90, 99-100, 113, 119
Amphetamine psychosis, 76
Anger
  in, 45, 50
  out, 45, 50
Anorexia, 95
Antisocial behavior, 56, 82
Anxiety, 38, 45, 62, 70, 98
Arousal, 32, 72
Arousal seeking, 92
Aspirin, 18
Asthma, 32, 34, 50, 94
Athersclerosis, 101
Audioanalgesia, 18, 21
Augmenting (see Reducing)
Autokinetic effect, 30
Autonomic balance, 11
Autonomic nervous system, 9
Avoidance learning, 65

B

Bedwetting, 59
Biochemical theories of schizophrenia, 73
Brain damage, 23, 39-40

C

Calorie intake, 99-100
Catecholamines, 78
Celibacy, 103
Civilization, 40
Classical conditioning, 17, 21-22, 55, 59-60, 65, 110
Climate, 103

Conformity, 30
Conscience, 59

D

Deaf, 16
Defense mechanism, 27, 30, 39
Delinquency, 17, 22, 49, 58, 114, 119
Delusions, 71
Depression, 25, 27, 45, 49, 56, 76
Differentiation, 29
Domestication, 40
Double bind theory, 70
Dreams, 30
Dysthymia, 22, 25, 32, 50, 81

E

Economic growth, 103
Ectmorphs (see Endomorphs)
Embedded figures, 29
Emotions, 6
Endomorphs, 24, 48, 65, 77, 95, 113
Exploratory behavior, 111
Extraversion (see Introversion)
Eye pigment, 39

F

Field dependence, 29, 39-40, 56, 71, 95, 113
Field independence (see Field dependence)
Figural after effects, 72, 81

H

Hallucinations, 68, 70
Heart disease, 101
Homicide, 88, 114
Hypertension, 32, 101
Hypochrondria, 16
Hysteria, 22, 50, 81, 114